Deep Paisley

a collection of stories, poems,
comments and theologies

Christopher M. Tweel

Parson's Porch Books
www.parsonsporchbooks.com

Deep Paisley: a collection of stories, poems, comments and theologies
ISBN: Softcover 978-1-949888-88-1
Copyright © 2019 by Christopher M. Tweel

All rights reserved. No part of this book may be reproduced or transmitted in any form or by any means, electronic or mechanical, including photocopying, recording, or by any information storage and retrieval system, without permission in writing from the publisher.

Cover design by *Room to Bloom, Illustrations*, Beth A. Conrad

For my wife.

Who listens endlessly to my rants and encouraged

a better sense of what the story was really all about.

Having you on our team changes my life each new day.

Contents

Essays and Biblical Reflections

Our Mother Who Art in Heaven 9
Living as a Christian in a Pagan Culture 12
The Little People 15
Jesus Whipped 22
A Duck 29
Model 35
Fall for Anything 41
Easy Rider 44
Free-Dumb 52
Let Freedom Bring 55
Life for Dummies 58
American Seams 60
Church and Drool 63
A Quiet Place 67
Builders 73
Be the Judge 79
The Cost of Christ 87
Dusty Teva's 92
Action Verbs 99

Poems

Oceana 106
Snowfall 110
Is it Fall? 111
Unkind Air 112
As I sit behind you 114
Ode to dead petals on my floor; dedicated to no-one 115
Will these fingers type ever faster? 117
Out Dancing 118
Shadeless Room 120

Smoke	121
Reflections	122
Moule Cafe	123
psalm 101	124
RSS Fed	125
A truth of zeros	126
Sock drawers	127
So scared	128

Short Fiction

Shift	133
Asspettere la Bella	147
Places	163
Trains	165
Let me off	167
Legacy	169

Essays and Biblical Reflections

Our Mother Who Art in Heaven

About a decade ago, there were rumblings throughout the Methodist church about a new aspect of " spirituality." Honestly, I was a little young to remember the specifics but there were a group of likeminded people "out west somewheres" (west of Ohio, where I was at the time) that were taking a new view of the sexuality of God.

Somehow, this is where God the Mother got some of the grounded foundation that began to grow in popularity. In college we had a Chapel Dean who would refer to God as "Her." It never really bothered anyone enough to do anything about it. My circle of friends just agreed that it wasn't what we were used to and sounded somehow foreign, yet in the truth of the matter God was genderless at God's core, so you could potentially refer to God as you chose.

The problem with all this arises when people, who are far less comfortable with their perception of God being altered, are confronted with the notion of God the Mother. Or, conversely, when an overzealous feminist latches onto the term in order to shove the female persona in the faces of a male dominated religion.

Unfortunately, I've had the displeasure of dealing with both types.

The first type are the ones who have been handed down traditions in the form of doctrine, which they assume was actually created by the hand of God on high. The problem here is that this inhibited way of thinking leaves no room for one of the most important parts of Christian life--the Holy Spirit--which was specifically left by Christ as a comforter and teacher in His physical absence. Jesus never asked his followers to close off their brains to new thought, nor did he reply to their questions with, "Well, I've always done it this way, that's why."

The ministry of Christ was one that was filled with tough questions and even tougher answers that came with them.

The second are even less predisposed to having a change of mind, however. I've met feminists who are boons to their sex and to the world because of how they choose to approach the

issues. And there are certainly issues out there that need champions. Sadly, as with all professions, there are those who craft a bad name for the collective, some of whom are the ones jumping on the "God is my Homegirl" bandwagon for no other reason than the sheer joy of being a thorn in the side of Strom Thurmond and Pat Robertson.

The bottom line is that God is neither--and both, and everything in between. First, if I may, consider these two pieces of scripture:

"O Jerusalem, Jerusalem, you who kill the
prophets and stone those sent to you, how often I have longed
to gather your children together, as a hen gathers her chicks
under her wings, but you were not willing (Matthew 23:37)."

This has Christ using obvious feminine allusions in regard to God; the motherly desire to gather the brood closely for protection and out of love. The other scripture is from Genesis 1:27: "And God created man in His own image, in the image of God, He created him; male and female He created them."

Clearly a description of God forming both sexes to reflect His/her own image. The only difficulty arises out of not being able to stretch our minds to the infinite nature of the Almighty even the least little bit. God has no gender and yet is both aspects of everything we perceive. Male and Female social rules govern so much of our day to day actions it becomes extremely difficult for most of us to separate them and disassociate ourselves from them in regard to our worship life. Though, in truth, the question here is, must we do that? It is not necessary to see God as androgynous in order to meet faithfully with your God nor is it compulsory for us to rewrite every piece of church tradition and service to reflect the non-gender that God owns. Only in our minds and hearts does the revolution need to take place.

If you are in need of your God as the Motherly comforter then so picture it. Our image does not change the Nature of God. If our life needs the strict guidance of the fair judge and Father,

then so be it. If Christ can liken His father to a hen, then shouldn't we be able to also allow ourselves the ability to see both sets of parents in the Infinite?

For most people this idea is not news, but for others it may still border on heresy. Mostly and conclusively the problem lies in our innate inability to match our mortal minds to the

infinitude that is God. The idea that a being could be both and neither, in the past and the future, is as near to an aneurism as most of us care to get.

So, we tirelessly revert to the one solid tangible thing that every believer of every sect can agree on. Father or Mother or Non-sexed, God is Love. It shouldn't be that hard for us to picture a being devoid of gender who loves us, but for many it is.

Living as a Christian in a Pagan Culture

Not too long ago (May 2003 edition, Parkersburg Sentinel) there was a brief article by Liz Grimes entitled "This is a Christian culture?" in reference to the culture of the US.

I suppose that I could see how, on the surface, one might think so. What, with these "Bible beaters" throwing "Merry Christmas" down our throats at every turn. And true, the US probably does still rate one of the more moderate television lineups when compared to the world at large. But puritanical values do not a Christian culture make.

The truth of the matter is that American culture is far from the values espoused in any sect of Christianity, and so many of the churches will tell you that off the cuff. As the social divisions become more and more apparent the truth behind our society rears its ugly head.

It seems that the lie begins sometime in the 1950·s when some people for the first time in their lives had disposable income, and the emerging TV media was there and waiting with a list of things that were needed in every American home. Somehow in that time purchases became synonymous with being a good, red-blooded, all-American W.A.S.P--the envy of every neighborhood. Mother and Dad and the kids dressed in fine things in the family Buick on the way to Sunday services. This is not Christian culture. Those are Christians living in American Culture.

Honestly, I'm really not sure that the majority of people in the US could survive a Christian culture. Christ promises that life will be hard! And, that His followers will be ridiculed. By converse thinking, does that mean that if you aren't finding it difficult to fit into society, then maybe you aren't following Christ closely enough? Being a Christian, a true follower of everything that Jesus stands for, is one of the most difficult practices there is. I had a favorite youth leader of mine that used to quote, "Mmm. Being; a Christian. Ain't for wimps!"

Unlike other religious beliefs, there is so much more to the faith than a simple doctrine of "reap what you sow." Not a basic tenant, but it is truly only one facet of the belief. There are in fact two more basic, intrinsic and infinitely more difficult ultimate guidelines: Love God with all your heart and soul and mind (which is numbing in its possibilities. What things in this life or this earth do we truly love so deeply? What is our frame of reference for this deed?), and the other, love your neighbor as you love yourself.

Now, simply to discuss in brief the last of these and, to ignore the idea of self-loathing, how difficult is this simple phrase in practice? I know from experience that it is tough to put even my spouse's desires above my own. Though I love her more than any other person on earth, my first response is to defend myself in arguments, to place my needs above hers. It is a battle not to do so! And yet I do, and I know that she does the same. And yet, as difficult as that is, as hard as we work and talk and understand one another, here is a command from

Christ to do that same work with every one of my neighbors. And if you understand that the realm of neighbor could potentially reach out of your neighborhood and touch stores that we frequent, friends and relatives, the list seems to spiral out of control. Is it even possible?

A Christian Culture is one in which every single person puts every other person ahead of their own desires. I know, much to my wife's chagrin, that I fail to do that with her on a weekly

basis, to say nothing of my actions to people outside my family. The other point that is important to consider is that goodness will never equal a Christian heart. It actually saddens me that

Christians and their habits are not more prevalent so that people are better able to identify Christian attitudes from ones that are simply "good."

Christians are people who strive, each hour of each day (pray unceasingly!) to set aside their own wishes, to lay down their own selfish humanity and to take on the easy mantle of servanthood, peace, and self-sacrifice. Christians too should "live as gently as possible on the Earth," if for no other reason than that God entrusted it to us as caretakers, it was given as a blessed gift for our sustenance. Any home gardener knows that you must care for the garden or it gives you weeds you can't eat.

So, instead of reclaiming, seek to dis-claim. Instead of finding things that serve us, seek to serve. A Christian culture is something difficult, seemingly impossible, without the miraculous effect of God's presence. But it is surely not something that exists today except in the minds of those who simply do not have an understanding of what that would be like.

The Little People

Romans 16:12-23 (CEV)
Greet Tryphaena and Tryphosa, who work hard for the Lord. Greet my dear friend Persis. She also works hard for the Lord. Greet Rufus, that special servant of the Lord, and greet his mother, who has been like a mother to me. Greet Asyncritus, Phlegon, Hermes, Patrobas, and Hermas, as well as our friends who are with them. Greet Philologus, Julia, Nereus and his sister, and Olympas, and all of God's people who are with them. Be sure to give each other a warm greeting. All of Christ's churches greet you.

My friends, I beg you to watch out for anyone who causes trouble and divides the church by refusing to do what all of you were taught. Stay away from them! They want to serve themselves and not Christ the Lord. Their flattery and fancy talk fool people who don't know any better. I am glad that everyone knows how well you obey the Lord. But still, I want you to understand what is good and not have anything to do with evil. Then God, who gives peace, will soon crush Satan under your feet. I pray that our Lord Jesus will be kind to you.

Genesis 22:1-14 (NIV)
Sometime later God tested Abraham. He said to him, "Abraham!" "Here I am," he replied. Then God said, "Take your son, your only son, Isaac, whom you love, and go to the region of Moriah. Sacrifice him there as a burnt offering on one of the mountains I will tell you about."

Early the next morning Abraham got up and saddled his donkey. He took with him two of his servants and his son Isaac.

When he had cut enough wood for the burnt offering, he set out for the place God had told him about. On the third day Abraham looked up and saw the place in the distance. He said to his servants, "Stay here with the donkey while I and the boy go over there. We will worship and then we will come back to you."

Abraham took the wood for the burnt offering and placed it on his son Isaac, and he himself carried the fire and the knife. As the two of them went on together, Isaac spoke up and said to his father Abraham, "Father?"

"Yes, my son?" Abraham replied.

"The fire and wood are here," Isaac said, "but where is the lamb for the burnt offering?"

Abraham answered, "God himself will provide the lamb for the burnt offering, my son." And the two of them went on together.

When they reached the place God had told him about, Abraham built an altar there and arranged the wood on it. He bound his son Isaac and laid him on the altar, on top of the wood. Then he reached out his hand and took the knife to slay his son. But the angel of the LORD called out to him from heaven, "Abraham! Abraham!" "Here I am," he replied. "Do not lay a hand on the boy," he said. "Do not do anything to him.

Now I know that you fear God, because you have not withheld from me your son, your only son."

Abraham looked up and there in a thicket he saw a ram caught by its horns. He went over and took the ram and sacrificed it as a burnt offering instead of his son. So Abraham called that place The LORD Will Provide. And to this day it is said, "On the mountain of the LORD it will be provided."

It's exciting when we feel that the scriptures written so long ago still have the resonance of truth in our lives today. We sometimes feel that this world in which we live is so drastically different from the one about which Paul was writing. Yet, here at the end of Romans, we find instruction that was originally meant for that church filled with loving instructions that we can still apply today.

First, we must bear in mind that the church in Rome was one that was truly near and dear to Paul's heart. In the previous lines of the reading, we hear of people who have been just like family, the words in verse 16 sounds almost like, give everybody a hug for me.

It is in this context that we are required to look at his last words of instruction for the new church. It boils down basically to three things:

    1) Watch Out!
    2) Keep yourselves focused
    3) Hold out for God's help

In the first place Paul tells the church to look sharp! And this goes beyond the boundaries of what we may initially consider. It is not a matter of NOT doing wrong, but of actively pursuing the right. I've heard people comment on the old adage that "if you can't say something nice then don't say anything at all." The Christian turn on that phrase would have to be, "If you can't say anything nice about someone, then tell them all the things you love about them." We fail sometimes to see that inaction can be equally as harmful as action.

My father is an immensely safe driver. Growing up and riding in the car with him I always felt safe. His focus was only on his driving no matter what else; hands at ten and two, blinker used at every turn; everything was by the driver's manual. One night, as he was driving to visit his mother in Huntington, WV, he dozed off at the wheel. Angels must have been with him. His car simply went into the median on the other side of the highway and stopped facing the opposite direction.

But there is our example. Sometimes inaction is just as if not more harmful than the wrong action. Technically my father did nothing during the accident (he was after all asleep and inactive), yet it could have been a great tragedy.

So here Paul is warning the church to stay awake at the wheel!

"Don't let troublemakers take root in the church community," he asks. One translation, at the end of verse seventeen says, "Keep away from them But, I enjoy a different translation which becomes, "Look sharply at them Not only keep your eye on them, but make it known that they are outside the community of faith with their actions.

In a way this goes along with Paul's second point, which is asking the church to stay focused on the goals at hand. They are there, not to serve themselves, but Christ; they have important work and Paul asks them to be truly concerned with that work and not with the flattery or fancy talk that the troublemakers bring.

In the last part of his wisdom, Paul talks of the God of peace "coming to crush the adversary." Hold out for God's work, this says. Hold out for His help in these matters. These people who "put stumbling blocks" before you will be dealt with by God or by His work. We can perceive the warning here: never act to try and protect our own pride, but instead keep an eye on those who would hinder the deeds of Christ with their attitude and let God's Will prevail with them.

It a hard distinction to make but an important one. It's the difference between doing our will and the Lord's. But why are these people here? So, even in the earliest days of the church there were those who, much to the chagrin of the other Saints, stood in the way of faith-led people taking action.

Or, was Paul's warning even deeper to include the leaders themselves? Perhaps the better question than "why are those people around?" is "how do we keep from becoming like them?" For the Why and for an understanding of those who would place the stumbling blocks in our path, we are in luck that our New Testament reading this week is matched up with the familiar Old Testament tale of Father Abraham.

My own father actually doesn't like this story very much at all. He has a hard time perceiving not only the act but why God would ever even ask it of Abraham in the first place. I suppose that as his son the fact that this idea is so foreign to him is comforting.

And it is a difficult story to read. Poor Abe! After years of waiting he is finally able to rejoice in the blessing of a son; the promise made so long ago has come to fruition but only for God to go and ask for the gift back! I am sure that I would not have been able to stand up to the task. Some can say that God is unfairly baiting Abraham, waiting for him to fail, hinging the promise on some gruesome act. Others would say that it is a test for Abraham, a monument to his faith if he is able to truly draw the knife across his son's throat. The latter, I think, is more correct.

It is a test, but here we have to understand the deep relationship that Abe and the Lord of Heaven shared between them. In essence, God tests Abraham even when he was a young man, commanding him to leave the valley of Ur and travel far to the west. And ever since his story started, he is tested again and again and again. God makes a most special promise to him and as the holder of the line; God must come to know Abraham intimately--to know Abraham better than his wife ever knew him; to know Abraham better than his own mother knew him. And God knows, of course, that action speaks so much louder than words. Not but a few weeks ago we read from the seventh chapter of Matthew, "Not everyone who says to me Lord, Lord will enter the Kingdom of Heaven." Honestly this all reminds me of the song Eliza Doolittle sings in My Fair Lady:

> Don't talk of stars burning above; If you're in love, Show me! Tell me no dreams filled with desire. If you're on fire, Show me!

And so, I can imagine God saying those exact same things. If you love me, show me. If you are on fire to do my will, show me. Thus has it always been for Abraham. What I meant when

I originally said that we must understand the relationship so as to understand the real meaning of the tests, was that Abraham's life wasn't really a test as we think of it, but more like all of our lives are: a succession of opportunities to show God our true heart. This is the only way he has of getting to know us-- with Abraham it is only more so. God will allow nothing to get between him and his chosen Steward of the Promise. If anything in Abraham's life is going to get in the way of God's Will, it is going to be his son.

The son who is the culmination of decades of waiting. The son who, to Abe at least, represents the entirety of God's promise to him. It is a symbol of their connection. But God is a jealous god and will let nothing be between them. So, the call comes out, "Give me your son." Show me. Understand here though that Abraham's love was not in question here, but instead, God questions the placement of his heart. Which is it? Your son and all he represents, or continual obedience to my Will; no matter what that may be--no matter if you will or won't understand it?

It's a hard question. And yet the same is asked of us every day.

In a thousand ways we are constantly provided with the opportunities to show our God how we love Him.

So why must we bear the troublemakers who divide the church? Because, they are only those who have come up short in the question of heart placement. And, yes, we are asked to separate ourselves from the doctrine of foolish talk that they come out with, but we are also commanded to watch them, for what is the true purpose of the church if not to take people when they fail the Test of Abraham and guide them and love them to more opportunities for continued reconciliation with God?

So we take Paul's last words of his letter to a beloved church, and we remember not to "fix" people as we see them in need, but we respond in love to them as God guides us to do. Because the last part of verse twenty echoes to us out of the ages: "I pray that Jesus will be kind to you."

He knows that we are the ones who are in need of the kindness of Christ in our daily failings. He reminds us not to become wrapped up in our role as a chosen people and to know that we are constantly reliant on Christ for our daily Grace.

To end we must also remember the last words that come as a warning from our friend Paul, and I will paraphrase, "Follow what I am asking of you, because sooner or later we are all on the receiving end of Grace, and in need of Christ's compassion."

Jesus Whipped

John 2:12-22 (NIV)
After this he went down to Capernaum with his mother and brothers and his disciples. There they stayed for a few days.

When it was almost time for the Jewish Passover, Jesus went up to Jerusalem. In the temple courts he found men selling cattle, sheep and doves, and others sitting at tables exchanging money. So he made a whip out of cords, and drove all from the temple area, both sheep and cattle; he scattered the coins of the money changers and overturned their tables. To those who sold doves he said, "Get these out of here! How dare you turn my Father's house into a marketplace!"

His disciples remembered that it is written: "Zeal for your house will consume me."

Then the Jews demanded of him, "What miraculous sign can you show us to prove your authority to do all this?"

Jesus answered them, "Destroy this temple, and I will raise it again in three days."

The Jews replied, "It has taken forty-six years to build this temple, and you are going to raise it in three days?" But the temple he had spoken of was his body. After he was raised from the dead, his disciples recalled what he had said. Then they believed the Scripture and the words that Jesus had spoken.

The temple in the time of Christ was an impressive structure. Remember that this is not the home for God originally built by Solomon. Created in a little over 46 years by "Herod the Builder" it was meant to inspire grandeur and wonder in the hearts of all those who passed before it. It was built in order to garner favor with the Jewish people. Historians who have studied it agree that, had it survived the Romans, it would have been one of the wonders of the ancient world.

The temple structure itself sat on a mounted area the size of twenty football fields. It was divided into three courtyards. The ancient historian Josephus wrote that the columns which were thirty feet high were so highly decorated that they "caused amazement to the spectators, by reason of the grandeur of the whole."

I will try to paint the picture in order to set the stage for our scripture. The tall structure is called the "The Holy Place" in which only priests were allowed to enter. This is what we see when we think of the temple proper. In the back of the "Holy Place" was the "Most Holy Place," in which only the High Priest was allowed to enter once a year. In front of the tall structure was the altar, where animal sacrifices were killed and burned. In front of the altar and Holy Place was a square courtyard for the Jewish women. Women were not allowed to enter the altar area. Non-Jews, i.e. Gentiles, were not allowed to pass through the temple walls at all, upon pain of death. There were tablets inscribed with promises to that effect surrounding the gates that passed from the Court of the Gentiles to the other Jewish courts.

In the scripture we had just read it was into this court, the Court of the Gentiles, that Jesus first passed. It had become traditional for the sacrificial animals be sold near the temple for a matter of convenience. Later, that tradition moved to inside the Court of the Gentiles. Usually the sellers were priests themselves, or family that the priest had allowed to rent space within the temple wall. In addition foreign coin was not permitted to be offered up to God in the temple offerings, so there were moneychangers who did the people the service of changing outside currency for the local breed--for a fee of course.

I need to convince you of something though, before going on. The Courts, including the Court of the Gentiles were all a part of the worship space. Say, as our sanctuary building is divided into (from the parking circle) the Portico, the Narthex, the Nave, and the Chancel--that's church lingo for the porch, the foyer, the sanctuary and the place where the pulpit is. Everything within the walls of the Temple Mount is considered to be holy ground, consecrated worship space, and the dwelling place of God.

It was this scene into which Christ walked. Imagine, the place of worship so profane, not only with the shouts of competitors hawking their particular sacrificial animal, but also with the smell of all those animals.

It enrages Jesus.

Growing up, we had kind of an unwritten rule in my mom's house about taking off your shoes at the door. I remember one time I went into an apoplectic fit when two of my friends marched up the stair with their boots on. Partly it was from fear of my mother, but it was also something else. It was also the fact that I did love my mother and didn't want to disobey a wish that she had. Well not this wish anyway. Christ here is the same. He calls the temple his Father's house on more than one occasion in the Gospels. And now, as he enters on what should be a time of worship and of coming together to witness God's provision, he sees the filth that the priests of the Lord have allowed the temple to become. How utterly angry he must have been! The tribe of Levi, entrusted with the most holy mission of bringing the will of God to the people, those who had a sacred trust, had instead made part of the house of God a fecal festival where the focus was on creating a profit.

As Christ's anger erupts, I again have a tape of the Disciples conversation going on in my head. Jesus comes in through the Gate of the Gentiles, into the Courts of the Lord. He silently

and grimly assesses the situation and then.

"Hey...uhm... Hey, Andrew, what's Jesus doin'?"

"Makin' a whip I think."

"Oh. Uh, why's he doin' that?"

"No idea."

"You gonna ask him?"

Andrew turns around slowly. "No. He's making a whip. You wanna be first? You ask him."

So, Jesus makes a whip. Probably something out of hempen rope that was handy. Nothing too serious, but, still a whip. The next passage in the text I think does a great job at understating the situation. It tells of how Jesus drove the people out of the Court of the Gentiles-- sheep and cattle and people and turned over carts, tables« lots of action going on there. The thing is, and this isn't stated because the author assumes, we know this already, but the passage doesn't tell you how big the Court of the Gentiles is. The whole complex is about twenty football fields. The Court of the Gentiles is the biggest single area in the whole complex. It's roughly about five football fields in size. Five. The scene in our imagination changes a little bit now. Before, it was maybe a few minutes of righteous fury, glorious in its brevity. Now, it is the systematic removal of people from an area of 2500 square yards. That takes a while.

Again the scripture lends itself to my overactive imagination.

It says the disciples recall the scripture, "Zeal for your house will consume me." (Psalms 69:9) I have them wide eyed and slack jawed, still standing near the gate where Jesus left them,

waiting out this terrible passion that Christ has, and then gaining a glimmer of understanding when he calls it "my Father's house," and being able to put the prophecy together with the prophesied.

This whole reading sticks out in our minds, and rightfully so. It is one of the few times we have any kind of anger indicated when regarding Jesus. Usually we have him pictured calming the waters, the soother, the healer. But here we get a glimpse of the righteous warrior. And we get a pretty clear message. There are some things you do not do. So many times in Jesus' ministry we can be a little confused at his actions because we forget how Jesus sees. He sees the heart. He cannot help it. The woman at the well is a great example. He views her heart before he sees one single facial feature, before he realizes she is Samaritan, or a woman. It is the same in the Temple Court. Upon entering he sees a different kind of filth. That of the greedy human heart. He sees the purpose that put those men in those booths, and it was not the desire for Godliness. It was not even the desire to provide for their families. It was their desire to take advantage of others and to put the almighty dollar, or shekel, before the promise of God. That was more offensive to him than all the dung and sweat in the whole of Israel.

We have here a stern warning. Sterner than the tablets that promised death to the Gentiles who dared to cross the line into the Jewish Courts of worship. From Christ it reads, "You come into my Father's house to worship? Then you better be darn sure that your heart is looking for Him and nothing else."

Christ doesn't expect us to come to the House of God with perfect hearts, or even with the best intentions. He took all kinds into his service as followers and healed all sorts of people in a vast array of afflictions. But what He will not tolerate are people who will not come as open supplicants before the sight of God. Or those who stand in the way of people who are. The house of worship is a place where we can let all our pretenses fall away before the sight of God: to lie stripped bare of every arrogance we allow ourselves during the week and say to God, "I have wronged your name; take me back; teach me again. I belong not to myself but to you and You alone." But, if we chose to enter these gates with hard hearts, with pride, with inflated self-worth, with ulterior motives, then we are only fooling ourselves until Christ is done making his whip.

Realize too that there are several more subtle ways in which we can abuse the Temple of God. Ways that are much easier for us to be tricked into doing so. Even something so simple as forgetting what worship is about abuses the Temple of God.

Just about what is worship. At the basic form, worship is what comes from our hearts to God. So often I think we get it wrong by expecting worship to be the fix in our weekly lives. We expect to come to worship and leave with a sense of wellbeing and peace. A sense that we can now face the week. But that isn't the purpose of worship. Sometimes that does happen, but it is a side note. It is the effect, the cause of which is our coming to God, our hearts ready for the right kind of worship.

If we leave with a sense of unease, or we feel as if it wasn't worth our time then we must consider the state of our own hearts as cause. Worship is not for us. It is for God.

Note here that the temple was called a house of worship--not a house of sacrifice, of offerings, or teaching, or prophecy, or even preaching. Everything done in the house of God is to lead to the worship of the Father--communion between our hearts and the Almighty.

We are left in this passage with a sense of hope. As you can imagine Jesus' actions created quite a ruckus in the workings of the temple and either the priests, or perhaps their family members who were working the booths, as Christ is giving them the heave-ho, ask Jesus "Who gives you the right to do this?"

Our hope is in His response, and look closely at what he says, "Destroy this temple, and I will raise it up." The "you" in that sentence is understood: You tear it down, I'll build it up. We are the destroyers. In the more literal sense he is speaking to his accusers, either in the crowd shouting for Barabas or in the council of the Sanhedrin. And, as the Bible is for all the ages,

He is also speaking directly to us.

No matter what we destroy, no matter what we fail, no matter the number of times our hearts break out of that stone, the Spirit of God comes flooding in all new and fresh, tearing down those walls we spent years painstakingly putting up. No matter how often that happens, Christ will always rebuild in our hearts anew.

So, in some ways we need to be periodically whipped by Christ. We need that anger to sweep through us and clear out that which is keeping us from the Temple of God. And most of all we need Christ to be there at the end of it, whip still in hand, saying, 'Go ahead. Do it again. I'll be here. You tear it down. And I will build it back up, better than ever Jesus truly is the Temple rebuilt. The place where in which we can worship and become reconciled to God.

This is the promise of Christ, and the will of a loving God who wants so desperately to be in the reality of our lives that He will allow himself to be, as the scriptures say, "Consumed with Zeal" for us and for the wish that our hearts be close to His.

A Duck

Mark 8:27-9:1 (NIV)
Jesus went on with his disciples to the villages of Caesarea Philippi; and on the way he asked his disciples, "Who do people say that I am?" And they answered him, "John the Baptist; and others, Elijah; and still others, one of the prophets."

He asked them, "But who do you say that I am?" Peter answered him, "You are the Messiah." And he sternly ordered them not to tell anyone about him.

Then he began to teach them that the Son of Man must undergo great suffering, and be rejected by the elders, the chief priests, and the scribes, and be killed, and after three days rise again. He said all this quite openly. And Peter took him aside and began to rebuke him. But turning and looking at his disciples, he rebuked Peter and said, "Get behind me, Satan! For you are setting your mind not on divine things, but on human things."

He called the crowd with his disciples, and said to them, "If any want to become my followers, let them deny themselves and take up their cross and follow me. For those who want to save their life will lose it, and those who lose their life for my sake, and for the sake of the gospel, will save it. For what will it profit them to gain the whole world and forfeit their life? Indeed, what can they give in return for their life? Those who are ashamed of me and of my words in this adulterous and sinful generation, of them the Son of Man will also be ashamed when he comes in the glory of his Father with the holy angels."

And he said to them, "Truly I tell you, there are some standing here who will not taste death until they see that the kingdom of God has come with power."

This first passage reminded me of a comedic scene that comes from a movie by Monty Python, a group of British actors who, among other things, created a movie about King Arthur's

Quest for the Holy Grail, the cup of Christ. It's a total spoof comedy and not meant to be serious in any way. The scene in particular that I thought of is one in which the people of a town bring a woman forward to be tried by one of the Knights for witchcraft.

Through a series of questions to the puzzled masses, Bedivere gets around to asking the public, "What else floats in water?"

Their replies remind me of a roomful of elementary students shouting out answers at random: "Beef gravy, churches, tomatoes, bread! Very small rocks!"

For some reason this is how I picture Peter, and maybe some of the other disciples throwing in their two cents about who the people thought Jesus was: "Elijah! John the Baptist! Nahum! Malachi! Obadiah!"

And then Peter, perhaps the favorite of the class, "You are the Messiah!"

Which to us at first seems right, yet, they are commanded not to tell anyone about it. To us, it is strange to hear the disciples silenced like this. It is odd to our ears for "Messiah" to be the wrong answer. Maybe we can say to ourselves that the time was not right. But to me, the mood behind what Jesus says is not, "wait then until the time is right," but a stern order not to tell anyone.

What then is the issue? In the following verses he begins teaching, first to the disciples, then to the crowds at large about what his last few weeks are going to be like. What brought this on?

It starts with the meaning behind their Messiah. To us it has much more meaning than it did to the disciples in that age. The word messiah, in the Greek is translated as "anointed one." Which, again we are at least familiar with as a synonym for

Christ. But in this perspective, it means something a little different. The disciples perceive the anointing through the only medium they know: the Hebrew Bible, our Old Testament. They have been taught this and discussed it since they were young men.

Kings were chosen by God through the service of anointing, an act which was to prepare them for their role not only as a political leader but also as high priest over all the tribes. This is the connotation that the disciples are trying to attach to Jesus. In their belief they pledge to him, "Truly you are the one who will be king and priest over us all!" And yet, they have misunderstood the true meaning of what Christ has come to do. We must perceive here that these questions are not at all asked on accident. On the road to Caesarea and Philippi Jesus is beginning to test them, the final exam is coming up, and so he begins the lesson review in order to prepare them for the thing he knows is coming. Even his questions are ordered in such a way as to bring teaching to them. Who does the world say that I am? Are they right? Who do you say that I am? Are you perceiving it truly enough?

Here in this first part of the passage we begin to see the set up. The following teachings will only echo the battle between the things of man versus the things of God.

The disciples, though, in this instance expect Christ to become that anointed King. And he tells them to keep their big mouths shut about it! Partly, because the time was not right, but also

because he knows that they are getting it wrong. That their understanding of what the Messiah will truly do is still clouded. So, he begins again and teaches them that he will be the truest meaning of messiah. What better King than the one who lays down his life for his people's lives? What better Priest than the one who teaches in words and in deeds?

The disciples expect him to be the king that they expect. A king that is only born of their historical and wholly earthly expectations. And for their answer and their expectations, Christ admonishes them. There is a word in Greek that is used several times in this reading -- epitimao. When translated it can come out as the word "rebuke," but its real meaning is slightly more subtle, with a much more enlightening implication. Truly its meaning has more to do with strong words that do not honor. Also it can mean that there is a judgment of sorts awarded here; a sense of understanding the merit of something and stating its proper place.

He talks then of suffering and even of death. Again it is harder for us to look at the disciples and followers of Christ with eyes of true empathy in this situation, since we know the end of the story. But for them the words were like an earthquake that had them reeling. Peter, their spokesperson, takes it upon himself to--remember this is the Greek word epitimao--rebuke or chastise Jesus for saying these things, we don't know the details, but perhaps we are able to imagine.

Jesus, a close friend, who has been a continuing source of wisdom and excitement for a group who before his coming were filled with disillusionment and fear. And now, after years of traveling together tells them of his impending doom? What are Peter's words? "Jesus, be kinder to us, isn't there another way? We will fight for you, there is no reason to lie down and die like a wimp!"

And whose words do these remind us of? At the beginning of Christ's ministry, we read about three instances in which Christ is tempted by Satan, who is trying to derail the entire purpose of who Jesus came to be. And here again, nearing the end of Jesus· ministry, using Peter as a mouthpiece, the Great Deceiver tries again to circumnavigate what must be done.

Christ answers for all to hear-- he despises not Peter in these words, but what Peter has said. I am reminded of my mother's and father's words growing up when I would act up, I love you dearly, but I hate what you are doing. Peter did not know, I think, that his words were against the will of God. We fall into the same trap--it is the trap of doing what seems to be "good" instead of what is truly Godly. Peter only wants to save his friends life. He wants to support and fight, he wants to work hard; put in the hours. Yet--Christ, in one of his most passionate moments openly condemns him in front of all the other followers. He says, I want you all to know that this is not going to work any other way.

And so we come fully into the real meat of these scriptures. Which way are we to choose then? God's way? Or the world's way? And further still we realize that the way of God is not always clearly the "good" thing. Many times it is the very thing that we cannot conceive of, that is the true will of God. Only with the discernment of the Holy Spirit are we able to tell the difference.

In the following lines Jesus expands on this same idea for the benefit of the crowd. There are times in scripture where I see Jesus reeling with certain things that he thought the disciples, at least, understood. Only to have them prove him wrong. I see him standing there going "What? I thought you guys knew this. Oh man... well, call the crowd together cause if you guys didn't get this then I know they didn't."

His words are not of strategic siege plans and the deposition of Herod Antipas, or of crushing debauchery with justice. What he says is even harder than those things. Deny yourself. Whatever it is that you are, deny it. He tells the crowd about what it really means to be a follower, a disciple of this man called Jesus.

We all know the old Bible adage that says, take up your cross. The beautiful part of that sentence lies within the Greek understanding in the translation. "to take up" in Greek is present imperative. In other words it carries the meaning of habitual moment by moment continuance. It's not a onetime thing; it is an alteration of habit. A lifelong moment by moment process.

As to the how of doing that we can return to the question on the roadway. Jesus is telling his followers that we cannot afford to believe what the world says. We cannot even trust our historical understandings. We may not even be able to believe our own sense of what is right and what is wrong.

Instead, he asks us to believe only what He gives us through the Holy Spirit. It's the only thing we can really trust in this life. Not the media, not the TV evangelists, not even our own selves. But only the truth that can come from the Spirit left to connect us with the Almighty.

Model

1 Thessalonians 1:1-10 (CEV)
From Paul, Silas, and Timothy. To the church in Thessalonica, the people of God the Father and of the Lord Jesus Christ.

I pray that God will be kind to you and will bless you with peace!

We thank God for you and always mention you in our prayers.

Each time we pray, we tell God our Father about your faith and loving work and about your firm hope in our Lord Jesus Christ.

My dear friends, God loves you, and we know he has chosen you to be his people. When we told you the good news, it was with the power and assurance that come from the Holy Spirit, and not simply with words. You knew what kind of people we were and how we helped you. So, when you accepted the message, you followed our example and the example of the Lord. You suffered, but the Holy Spirit made you glad.

You became an example for all the Lord's followers in Macedonia and Achaia. And because of you, the Lord's message has spread everywhere in those regions. Now the news of your faith in God is known all over the world, and we don't have to say a thing about it. Everyone is talking about how you welcomed us and how you turned away from idols to serve the true and living God. They also tell how you are waiting for his Son Jesus to come from heaven. God raised him from death, and on the Day of Judgment Jesus will save us from God's anger.

My parents both grew up in a city in WV named Huntington. My mother's father was a chemical engineer at a nearby nickel processing plant, and my father's father owned a soda fountain and sundries store in the downtown area. Growing up my dad's family never even owned a car, living downtown there was no need for one; my mother was the girl in her family in a largely patriarchal time and in addition, I'm not sure that her father knew anything to teach her about cars regardless. So my brother and I grew up without the knowledge, though I remember many times my brother, dad, and I would go to car shows at the mall and ogle at the sleek designs. Cars were appreciated, but more for their aesthetics than their engines.

By the time I was thirteen or fourteen, I took the fascination with the chasse to a different level. I started making model cars. Not running models, mind you; however, even those plastic ones had an engine you were required to assemble, to some degree, and I was able to come out of it with a rudimentary knowledge of the inner workings.

At least enough to stand in front of a temperamental vehicle with the hood up and stare thoughtfully into it. "Well, you see ah, that's the serpentine belt, and that looks ok. And that's your oil filter down there, and the air filter. This is where the spark plugs are, alternator..."

"So do you know why it won't start?"

"Nope. Not a clue."

I think that most people, perhaps men especially, think that people will assume you know what you are doing if you stare thoughtfully at something long enough.

But models can be pretty good at teaching us. We can perhaps remember some sort of physiology model from our classroom days, the human torso, or the human eye. In something of that same way, we can learn from this lesson that Paul has written about the church of Christ.

For a little background on the text, let me tell you that Thessalonica was the capital of Macedonia, which was one of the two Grecian provinces the Romans had established. The northern one was Macedonia and the southern one was

Achaia. The church was fairly early in its time away from Paul, who had fled the city to avoid persecution, thinking that the church would be better off. What happened was much the opposite, and the church there is one of the most persecuted.

Yet, at the time of Paul's writing the church was flourishing. In later passages, Paul says that the church is our (meaning he and Silas and Timothy) glory and joy and in several passages, he seems just to be reminding them of things he knows that they knew. There is a point where he states, "on the teachings of brotherly love--you have no need of them!"

We are in luck to be studying the first part of this passage that basically outlines for us the point of pride that Paul feels in this church. According to Paul this is a model church, and he goes on to describe four benchmarks that are part of what makes them such.

(1) It starts in earnest with verse 6. "And you became imitators of us and of the Lord." This is the aspiration of every preacher, pastor, deacon, elder, and member--all Christians strive to become true imitators of the true source. Martin Luther dubbed believers "little Christs," the connotation in German being that we should basically be "chips off the old block." To me, and my warped science fiction loving brain, I think of it as a genetic sample. Every genetic sample of any person or living things keeps, in fact, the entire genetic code of the original. If we then, being creations of the living Christ, pieces of His makeup, we should retain the entire code of behavior and ethics.

Of course in reality it is only through continuing study and the leading of the Holy Spirit that we can discern the nature of Christ, and oftentimes this may involve heavy revision in our thinking from time to time. So, in the first point Paul shares with us that the model church has ministers -- a job for all believers, not just ordained clergy -- who preach the word, live it and dwell within the Holy Spirit, as we know Christ and Paul did.

(2) Immediately after that Paul hands us the second aspect of the model church. "...for you received the word in much affliction, with the joy of the Holy Spirit." The BBE translation of the Bible states that "after the word had come to you in much trouble, with joy in the Holy Spirit."

What this boils down to is the persecution the church is suffering. Christianity was not an easy religion in those times. I find it most difficult to imagine not only the theological and life changing implications of a life as a Christian, but also to heap upon that the physical hardship or doing it behind the Romans' backs. If you have ever traveled to China or Russia before the fall of Communism, there is a taste of what the Thessalonians are dealing with daily. And yet, we find that they are not only receiving the text and embodiment of the Word of God but are also finding joy in doing so.

I am often shammed by the actions of people in countries much less prosperous than my own. When I first graduated college some of my family and I went to Palestine to see Bethlehem and some of the other holy sites. While we were there, we also visited an acquaintance of my who was a Melkite priest in a town named Iblin. Over the past ten years or so he had built a school there, during a time when the Israeli government was destroying not building.

He went through channels and got the required permits and his school now thrives. While we were there, I met a girl who was graduating with high honors and hoped to attend a college in Europe. Later the priest told us that she and her brothers walked six miles one way through two security checkpoints to get to school. It took them nearly two hours, four hours total a day. I was never more embarrassed of my 3.8 average than I was at that moment.

So it is with the early church. They are dealing with a strife and life of secrecy that we will never know, yet they do it anyway-- and more they meet it with joy. We in the church today know persecution as well, but to compare with my friend in Palestine, I too had to walk to school growing up as she did -- it took me six minutes at the most.

(3) The third piece of our puzzle is that the members of the church in Thessalonica are a blessed example. Paul says that they "...became an example to all believers in Macedonia and Achaia." Remember that these are the two provinces of Greece. North and South. Paul then goes on to say that their "...faith in God has gone everywhere, so that we need not say anything, for they themselves report..." The word is out about the church in Thessalonica! Being the lamp on the lamp stand, giving light to the whole household is an integral part of being the model church. Paul has internalized the truth of Christ's teachings and knows that a healthy church of Christ is not complete, or whole, or righteous unless they are a beacon to the rest of the world of everything that God holds dear. As Paul describes it, he doesn't even need to pick up a newspaper or get an e-mailed report about the things that the church there in Greece is doing -- he hears it from everyone.

For the span of Christ's teachings, by that I mean the assumed three years he was in ministry on earth, we have relatively little to go by. That can only mean that every word we have is

precious and written and said with power and the spirit behind them. Christ makes not one but two separate examples of the Christians' duty to the world: Illuminate it--Flavor it!

When it's pitch dark out and someone flicks on a light, you know it's there --you can zero in on it immediately! When you are cooking and leave out the salt--you know that it's missing!

These are the instructions for each Christian and the early church: be known in the world; make the world miss your presence when you are gone; be something that the world yearns for.

(4) The final note is one concerning God's sovereignty. Paul tells of how the church "...turn[s] to God from Idols to serve..." John Walvoord in 1973 made the note that the order of the phrase in Greek dictates that Paul meant the people of the church turned to God first, and then turned from their idols.

This is the only way that we as individuals can come into the power of God. We must never wait on our own goodness. We cannot try and persevere to be better people before coming to God or the church. That is a reliance on our own power and a profanity to the nature of our faith.

Instead, we must turn to God first, allowing His power to not only transform us but to strengthen us, from within--from the wellspring of His power. Then, with that in our spirits, turn from the daily idolatry with which we deal. To do any less would be like taking a beautiful piece of cherry wood to a master cabinet maker and then, while he waits, picking away burs or nettles or sanding imperfections that you think you see in the wood. We will never have the Master's eyes for the wood. Only God's expertise can bring the truest beauty of the grain to the surface in a sturdy useful structure.

These four things then have earned the church of Thessalonica the praise of Paul. In his absence, the church is still thriving, still holding to the precepts that he laid down for them: meeting in joy, receiving the Word of God, being examples to all others, and accepting God in the midst of their imperfections with truth and the want for a closer kinship with God.

Fall for Anything

"Kids today." It's an old trope. In the wake of the most recent school shootings, I asked a friend of mine what was different -- even now -- from the time we grew up. What was this insane virus that seemed to be spreading across the globe and has our children killing each other? They seem to be picking up guns and grenades younger each year. Each new event happening in the last places we thought safe.

I'm sure that some of it has to do with the fact that these are small towns and easier to make a big story of, but my friend replied something different than the simple herding of social media. She said, without hesitation, "It's the way they are raised."

Now, I know that we can't always go around blaming the parents for everything, however, these are, after all, just kids. A lot of kids are growing up today without that strong handed reprimand that I know was the custom in my family. There were certain things that were implanted into my head from day one, and each of these were enforced with some amount of vigor. But something a little stronger is infesting the hearts of these children. It's driving them to shoot classmates at point blank range, and at the end of it all, to shoot themselves.

The death count goes down from twenty to fourteen and somehow, we all feel relieved. Somehow fourteen kids killed so gruesomely is easier to handle than twenty. What we see as insanity is happening all around us. And months from now, unless the media feeds us reminders, we will forget whatever children perished beneath the call of our normal lives and duties.

Our children are being ignored. The boys that went in and killed their own classmates in Colorado were ignored. On Larry King he had guest that once said in regard to this, "No one does this out of the blue. There are always warning signs." It simply means that there isn't anyone who cares to witness them.

People probably saw them and were just too afraid to do anything. There were teachers who were afraid to report strange behavior; for the fear of having a parent-teacher encounter and perhaps losing their jobs for being "out of line," with accusations, because we are so anxious and defensive we have forgotten how to talk to one another with real care, and to hear concern as love. Parents who didn't want to admit their boys needed help, ignored the way they talked around the house. And due to the fact that not one person was brave enough to step forward, those boys got worse, formed a cohort, and ended the lives of themselves and their classmates. We in the U.S. are supposed to be the educated elite. We, as persons of Faith, are supposed to stand up for the meek and the mild. We as modern humans are supposed to concern ourselves with social injustices.

Do we? Or do we end up complaining about who won a contest that no one will remember in a few years. Do we fight for the injustices of the minorities? Or do we complain about the food we eat and how hard our lives are? As an educated public we have a responsibility to ourselves and to each other to stand up for what we have learned. Or are we not truly that educated?

We have a duty to find something that means the world to us personally and to seek it out, to fight for it, to not back down in the face of bureaucracy or the idiot mind of the dissociative wealthy class.

Because that is how we get defeated. When we listen to the "voice of reason" and not to our heart's innermost instructions. If you believe in something, if you believe in standing up for it, then do it. The whole idea of being alive is so that we become better thinking, passionate adults who will care about this place in which we live--and about each other. The idea here is that we cannot ignore the injustices around us. If you witness and event that sparks the ire of justice within you, take a stand; fight for the rightness you feel is there, and don't let those who have forgotten what real truth feels like stand in your way. Yes, the truth hurts, it stings and burns, but the reality that it represents is not to be compromised. The thing that made America a great nation years ago was the solidarity of spirit that the country was capable of feeling. Even know, even with a country so large and morally unwieldy it is possible if we are willing to come to terms with the basics of human justice. Even though the reality may be a world that is filled with injustice it is the universal belief and the attempt to reach that justice that make us stand together with pride in who our country is and represents. And that is very attainable if we are only willing to stand up and make it so.

Easy Rider

Luke 10:1-11 (CEV)
Later the Lord chose seventy-two other followers and sent them out two by two to every town and village where he was about to go.

He said to them, 'A large crop is in the fields, but there are only a few workers. Ask the Lord in charge of the harvest to send out workers to bring it in. Now go, but remember, I am sending you like lambs into a pack of wolves. Don't take along a moneybag or a traveling bag or sandals. And don't waste time greeting people on the road. As soon as you enter a home, say, 'God bless this home with peace.' If the people living there are peace-loving, your prayer for peace will bless them. But if they are not peace-loving, your prayer will return to you. Stay with the same family, eating and drinking whatever they give you, because workers are worth what they earn. Don't move around from house to house. If the people of a town welcome you, eat whatever they offer. Heal their sick and say, 'God' kingdom will soon be here!' But if the people of a town refuse to welcome you, go out into the street and say, 'We are shaking the dust from our feet as a warning to you. And you can be sure that God's kingdom will soon be here!'

Galatians 6:1-16
My friends, you are spiritual. So if someone is trapped in sin, you should gently lead that person back to the right path. But watch out, and don't be tempted yourself. You obey the law of Christ when you offer each other a helping hand. If you think you are better than others, when you really aren't, you are wrong. Do your own work well, and then you will have something to be proud of. But don't compare yourself with others. We each must carry our own load.

Share every good thing you have with anyone who teaches you what God has said. You cannot fool God, so don't make a fool of yourself! You will harvest what you plant. If you follow your selfish desires, you will harvest destruction, but if you follow the Spirit, you will harvest eternal life. Don't get tired of helping others. You will be rewarded when the time is right, if you don't give up. We should help people whenever we can, especially if they are followers of the Lord.

One of my good friends had a great grandfather in his family who was a Methodist circuit rider. His father still keeps his original saddlebags in excellent condition on display in the living room. His father ended up being a Methodist minister as well, oddly enough, so the bags were of special significance. A circuit rider was the original American Missionary. During the 1800's, they traveled on horseback a path that took them from small town to small town, and in most cases traveled routes that would take them nearly two months to complete. They took the words Luke to heart, taking only what they could carry in a pair of saddlebags as their only worldly possessions. In our society such simplicity of living seems almost unreal. They led lives of hardship as Peter Cartwright describes autobiographically in 'A Methodist preacher:' "when he felt that God had called him to preach, instead of hunting up a college or Biblical Institute, hunted up a hardy pony, and some travelling apparatus, and with his library always at hand, namely, a Bible, Hymn book, and Discipline, he started, and with a text that never wore out nor grew stale, he cried, 'Behold, the Lamb of God, that taketh away the sin of the world.'

In this way he went through storms of wind, hail, snow, and rain; climbed hills and mountains, traversed valleys, plunged through swamps, swollen streams, lay out all night, wet, weary, and hungry, held his horse by the bridle all night, or tied him to a limb, slept with his saddle blanket for a bed, his saddle-bags for a pillow. Often, he slept in dirty cabins, ate roasting ears for bread, drank buttermilk for coffee; took deer or bear meat, or wild turkey, for breakfast, dinner, and supper. This was old-fashioned Methodist preacher fare and fortune." It was a hard calling to be that kind of preacher, and still is. In a lot of little Appalachian communities the circuit, or charge-preacher, is still prevalent. I went to school with a fellow who is now a four-charge preacher, meaning, he has four churches to pastor. This, as you must imagine, can get a little difficult at times. He commented; it was "like being a stray dog at a whistlers' convention."

Though, sometimes I think we must thrive off difficulty. I was guilty of it so many times in college. Putting off a paper until the last night, as if just writing it wasn't challenge enough, I needed the added incentive of typing 25 pages in one sitting. There are also times in the spirit however, in which we try to make them harder than they need to be. One example is in the study of the scripture. I've heard students come to me many, many times after having wrestled with certain pieces until it just nearly drives them insane. One of the best pieces of advice I ever read is that, when dealing with scripture, don't get bogged down. There is a lot going on in almost every one of the passages here, and they are filled with meanings and sometimes social connotations that we just don't get on the first or second or third or twentieth reading.

Instead, we need to allow scripture to be the spiritual beast that it is and allow it to speak to us. If there is something we might not quite get, there is no shame is setting it aside, letting it rest, and coming back later. Yet, there is some part of us that thinks that if we worked harder at it, thought harder at it we would gain understanding.

There is a story from 2 Kings 5, about a general in the Ancient Syrian Army who was deeply troubled by leprosy. Now, he was used to hardship out on the field. He was used to boot camp, and army rations, and orders that were tough to carry out. The Bible also says that he was used to winning. Now this alone should tell us something about Naaman. It tells us a lot about the kind of man that he is. And yet, we can perhaps also imagine the degree to which his leprosy was afflicting him. This is a man who was used to battle wounds and scars and pain that has to go ignored and untreated until the task is finished. And yet, he was so undone by this disease he goes to his King to beg leave to travel down into Israel.

He is granted leave and goes first to the King of Israel but finds his way to the household of Elisha. He goes there in full pomp, and why not, he has earned his honored rank and title. His chariots and horses go with him and as he comes to the gate of Elisha's house a servant greets him. The servant gives him a message that if he is to be cured that he should go and wash in the Jordan.

This proved to be too much. Not only was the master of the house not going to meet with him (this is just after he has met with the King remember), he tells him to wash in the Jordan. Which, while it held a lot of significance it was still a river that was used for all kinds of things. Naaman doesn't actually come out and say that it's dirty but I think he implies it as he complains and rails at having to go bath in it. See, Naaman doesn't want the easy solution. He doesn't trust it. He thinks it won't work, that it's just a waste of time and he is bitter about the trip he took to get there. He is angry with the prophet and angry with himself for being taken in by the idea that his help would come from the Lord. A knowing servant came and pleaded with him, saying, "What could it hurt?"

But how like all of us is this proud general? How many times in life do we look to the hard road because the easy seems too good to be true? Sometimes the call to personal ministry doesn't seem difficult enough and so we refuse it or undermine it before we have ever even attempted it.

Christ sent out a call to his Disciples. It's a simple message. He asks that the disciples bring a message of peace, and the message of His divinity. No enormous messages of intricate faith, no mysteries of the cosmos revealed. Much to their credit they comply with the simple message and meet with success.

Much like the circuit riders of old, what did they have time for but to bring some of the most basic messages to the common folk of the mountains? It's very hard to run a sermon series on the finer points of living when you only see a particular church once in every six weeks.

Yet there is something heartwarming in coming to grips with the simple message -- and the simple charge. Paul has something here at the beginning of chapter 6 that is also easy in its simplicity; instructions on how to deal with the common sinner.

Paul knows that the church is Galatia is a trying church and perhaps in their overzealousness to find and perform the will of Christ, they have been a little too harsh with some of the brothers and sisters who have been tempted and succumbed. So many things being with good intentions and end up spiraling into a witch-hunt, trying to find someone to blame for it all.

Note too that here, no sin is specified. Paul does this purposefully to exercise the point that action for the person does not change according to the sin. It could be the foulest thing imaginable to man or a casual gray and innocent action. The reply should be the same. We are to approach the brother or sister in a spirit of meekness. Never, never, never in the Bible will there be ascribed an action of superiority when dealing with a weaker believer or outright sinner. The spirit of meekness is one that makes us self-evaluate beforehand and see with our own hearts our nothingness before the cross. Paul specifically asks for this confession in verse 3. We are to be prepared to bear one another's burdens, and, in verse 5, we are to realize our own responsibility. This last verse seems at odds with the previous verse as far and sharing burdens goes, but it is talking about our own understanding of taking responsibility for our actions in regard to this sinner. If we meet a sinner with condemnation and rebuke, then we will have to bear the burden of those consequences.

And is this really asking so much? The only thing that it denies us is the ability to be spiritual bullies. Lording our own righteousness against someone who has yet to find that peace. And maybe we can say that we would never think about doing that, but I might surprise you to say that the majority of the unchurched wholly expect it from us.

But this is an easy thing. To meet those suffering with sin with open humility and a readiness to help them shoulder the burden of their actions. Be ready to visit, to talk, to smile, and weep.

Jesus sends out the disciples into the very homes of people to share the Good Word with them. I know that whenever we have houseguest there is open conversation. A dinner together, a favorite dessert... I know that the disciples, who went out, knew and loved those people they stayed with in openness and humility. Jesus says to approach the mission field like lambs to symbolize that meekness.

And what is their reward? What do they reap from these actions? The submission of the evil spirits plaguing those people. Aside from that they returned with a joy in their hearts. That is the power that comes from this easy way of living. And even now I know there are some of us who are still skeptical. We still say, surely it must take more than that. If I have peace, and give peace, accept who Christ is, meet sinners with humility and a preparedness to shoulder some of the load... the return on that is joy and power over evil in the Name of Christ? There must be more to it, we say. And so we invent ritual, we make pomp our shield and traditions our armor. We say, there, this enormous laundry list of actions is what is really required of a Godly life. Now this complex belief system, that is what it takes. When the reality just isn't so.

Hopefully somewhere we hear the voice of Naaman's servant. Who whispers and says, "The answer is easy. Why not just try it?"

We have a real call from Christ. In Luke 10 at verse 1 it makes a point of saying there were 70 disciples sent out. That number has a message. It is the same number that Genesis chapter 10 uses to tell us the generation of Noah's family, the tribes of the world. It is also the number of men who sat on the Sanhedrin, the ruling council of the Jews.

In this number Jesus is telling us that the message is to go to the entire world, and that we will have the authority to back that message up.

So we receive this call, to seek the world, not all at once; the idea is to get the understanding that what we have isn't for the select. It's for every one of our neighbors and co-workers and friends and family and classmates. Additionally we know that we have the authority to back up the claims we make on Christ's behalf.

Maybe it's about time we did something that was easy. Faith becomes another burden to be checked off the laundry list of items we keep. Jesus says that we should be joyful not because we have power over spirits, but because we have received salvation. That understanding can be very freeing in our lives if we allow it to be. It was meant to be.

If we can alter our perception of, even our own church family, so that we don't see a pasty white school marm with a ruler standing over our heads ready to crack us on the knuckles every time we sin, we'll be better off. Instead, imagine friendly Paul, sitting in our home, listening patiently to our self-examinations, and our confessions, maybe kindly saying, you know such and such is a wrong way to live, will you let me help you with that? Wouldn't you feel a lot more like confessing? Hard work is a definite virtue. But sometimes Christ intends the easy road for us to follow. Our anger and our pride can get in the way of that, but the cleansing that is there for us to receive is worth us letting go of those false gods. Only then can we accept the easy call that Christ has for each of us, the call to go to people, some who will be brothers and sisters in the faith, and some, who will be strangers to God, but people and therefore His Children. But to go to them, and meet them with humility, share their burden, and renew the acceptance of Christ.

That is the kind of easy living that is going to lead us into a life of daily joy and empowerment in the Spirit; that kind of easy living makes the church a stronger place for being able to meet one another with real burden-sharing humility. And more than those it creates a life that lives actively in the Salvation that God has provided for us.

Free-Dumb

Don Surber, a syndicated editorial columnists, asks in a recent article why some people "seem to hate the U.S." Applaudably he lists many of the characteristics that make this nation one of the greatest in the world--in the same breath, however, he fails to mention any of the actions of our country that should shame all of its citizenry.

There are a number of reasons why people could hate what the United States has done. All you need to have is a mind that is tuned in any way toward social justice or have family and friends in any number of second and third world countries that the US makes a habit of exploiting for its own egocentric gain. Look at what has happened within our own borders. Aside from the Muslim community in our nation being bitterly disappointed by our president's nature to vacillate once in office on issues on which he promised a hard line, they have had to endure treatment that under any other circumstances would have been labeled prejudiced and criminal.

An article from the Associated Press stated "...the federal government has detained hundreds of immigrants, closed U.S. Muslim charities suspected of terrorist ties and gained broad powers to monitor citizens under the US Patriot Act." Also, in 2005, in northern Virginia, Muslim people who were community leaders and respected businesspeople had their homes and workplaces raided by Homeland Security officers in an effort to find links for terrorist funding operations. Raids on civilians? Military detainment? Bigotry? These actions fly in the face of the freedoms that we strive so hard for. A part of me is waiting expectantly for the day when Muslims of all types will be pushed into concentration camps, much like the US did for the Japanese Americans during the Second World War. The treatment of our citizens since the Twin Towers tragedy has been nothing short of racial scape-goating.

The authors of many newspaper and magazine articles have taken to denouncing anyone who questions the authority of the government or its decisions in their writings. What a waste!

For, in those statements, those people truly reveal to us all how little of the concept of Freedom they understand. Freedom is not acquiescing to the rule. Freedom is questioning. Freedom is that ability we all have to cry out when we feel that injustice has been served. We can call out at our nation itself and say, "Prove your actions to me. I demand it." Our country isn't Perfect -- and it is only by occasionally holding our system accountable that we will have a chance of achieving even more than already has been achieved. As citizens, we owe it to our country to disagree with it from time to time. In addition, we have the responsibility to let our disagreement be known. So, I answer Surber's question. Why do some people hate the US? They hate us because they fear us. They fear us because they look at our past and see that we are a nation that acts time and time again out of our own ignorance and fear. They see the evil that we have wrought and will not recognize. They see arrogance in our movies and, yes, in our news media. They see that we in our own country cannot be at peace with one another. They see people that have been citizens and neighbors for years who are now sometimes regarded as suspects. As a nation, we are like teenagers. We are young, strong, vibrant, and filled with new and wonderful ideas. We, as a people, can tend to be highly intelligent but horribly uninformed. The older nations, our parent nations, fear for us because with our youth comes a self-destructive belief that we are immortal--unconquerable.

To end, I pose still other questions: what do you do with a nation that holds so much power and so little temperance? How do you inject prudence and thoughtfulness into a people who have none? Is it even possible to turn the tide of assiduous fear once it has begun its terrible march? Hopefully we will be able to answer these questions and still keep intact the original spirit of this nation that, at one time, promised to make it a great one.

Let Freedom Bring

The other day I was reading an article published in the Charleston Gazette newspaper, published in 2003. Leonard Pitts, Jr., an author for another paper whose column got picked up by the Gazette, posed the question "Today it's black men in New York City; tomorrow it's who, and where?" He was referring to three unarmed black men who were shot to death by members of the NYPD. It's a tragic story, but Pitts' approach to the longer reaching effects of behavior like this is wrong. His point is that these officers will not contain their "miserable behavior" on one side of the tracks, and he asks what there is to stop them from getting away with it on the other side. He also says that it is everyone's problem.

Unfortunately, he is wrong.

While it is true that police brutality may someday break the bonds of race, giving a new and perverse meaning to equality under the law, one boundary that will never be broken is the boundary of class. Pitts stated this himself. He says that this sort of behavior is currently on "that" side of the tracks. Historically, violence has always been more dominant in the more economically challenged sections of towns and cities, which in the U.S. usually means the parts of town where people of color statistically reside. In the same light, this is where most of the police brutality cases occur. The simple answer to the question, "why," because they can. If the officers in question were tried for brutalizing someone of a higher income bracket, say, a bank owner, there would have been no acquittals. The reasons are as old as democracy itself. It stems back to one of the oldest problems of a republican system (i.e., a republic; not a reference to the partisan title) which is that essentially there is a mob rule. While I am not advocating a disposal of the government, I am pointing out what many people see as "unfair." The truth of the matter is that in the justice system, the people sometimes get in the way. There is a network of supports and politicos who favor or disfavor a certain side. All of it though is essentially to try to keep a certain part of the public happy: the part that votes -- which is predominantly 'upper-class' suburbanite, white males, and the elderly. This is why you don't see many senators in the slums campaigning to the hookers. Maybe once in a while, a political figure will go down to the "dregs" and show his shining white face, but usually this is only in order to appeal to some of the more liberal suburban white males who believe they need a man who will represent all the people, though even this is only to gain the favor of that same elite group. Because even if those in these places do vote, the power structure does not reside there in the way that wealth responds to racism. The connection between wealth and racism is as old as the money made from the slave industry, which is to say every cent of "old" money made before the end of the civil war.

I really do hate to shatter Mr. Pitts' ideals that the corrupt system would somehow leak out of the hood, but in truth it will not. The officers understand where they can and cannot get away with something akin to brutality or their own racist interpretation of the law. The real sorrow is that simply voting in these areas of unrest will not ease the socially unjust burden that they carry. There are only two ways of alleviating the problem, and they have very little to do with voting. One, if there is a large corporation in the area that donates heavily to campaigns (you'd be amazed at how safe the tobacco industries grounds are), or two, if some humanitarian political leader takes a particular interest in the area (which could be for personal or profitable reasons).

So, unfortunate though it is, the same democratic and capitalistic problems will forever plague areas of our societies. I sincerely wish that police and civil brutality would leak out into the other arenas of society: That honestly is the measure of equality. However, until then, money talks, and freedom rings -- as long as you're white, or sub-urban, or wealthy.

Life for Dummies

There was a cartoon in the local newspaper the other day that was spoofing books that seem to cater to the less intelligent members of society. What I am referring to is, of course, *The Idiot's Guide to...* and the *...For Dummies* series. The strip reads through several titles along the same lines in an effort to drive the joke; Shakespeare for Stupids, Music for Morons, and Philosophy for the Primitive. The punch line was that the patron went to the desk of the bookstore and asked if there were any books for the 'reasonably well informed.'

While the cartoon was funny, and while the "for Dummies"' series is not a bad reference for beginners on a variety of topics, there is one issue that everyone seems to overlook. They are calling us stupid.

We have all spent years in the defence of our intelligence through grade school and beyond; we were ready to take up arms against the first person that would dare call us names. Yet in our society today we buy books that are blatantly calling us names. Maybe I am taking the simple title of a self-help book out of context, but I find that this actually reflects a larger issue.

While some Far Eastern, European, and Middle Eastern countries are experiencing brain drains as more and more of their top scientific minds leave the country seeking more profitable employment, America too is having its own form of the global "dumbing down." However, our descent into idiocy is much subtler.

American culture has been progressing this way for years with schools taking more time to 'prepare' students for national tests as opposed to ensuring that the student will actually learn and retain information.

We have taught ourselves not how to learn and adapt, but how to take tests, how to beat the system, and how to make ourselves look attractive in interviews. We are a society that has been built up on tips and tricks instead of knowledge and know-how. It's no wonder we can so readily admit that we are still, basically dummies, seeing as how we know that, everything we claim to know is just a smokescreen carefully crafted through our years in public education and universities.

More and more we are becoming a country with an ever-widening gap between the 'knows and the 'know nots.' Instead of an economic gap, we have begun the long trail into an intelligence gap. The trend we are setting is going to lead us into having a society that will depend on having service members who add a human element to the mega-corporations and automated machines that have taken over all industrial labor. The majority of people will need to know little more than marketing schemes and consumerism.

The greatest provider of this kind of life is mass media, of course. More and more people are being fed through the television every day, and are essentially being programmed not to think, but to absorb. To numbly take in the information that the television media decides to throw out across the airwaves. Somehow, the television has fooled us all into believing that we can learn everything we need to know from the set.

In essence, the comic strip was issuing a serious warning under a tongue-in-cheek guise. we've all got brains ready to act upon anything we set it in motion to do. Get busy thinking' or get busy dyin'.

American Seams

It seems like in the past few years there have been a lot of, well, let's say disgruntled people, in our country. There have been the staunch divisions seen and revisited a hundred times. The effects of the blue and red marked map of our land are burned into our minds. The feelings of unity that the country might have shared at one time seem shattered, and now as the National Holiday approaches I hear whisperings that we don't have much to celebrate this year.

In places all over the country, we hear either the hard-liners, who believe whatever the government says patriotism and the depressing embarrassment of those who might claim to be

Canadian when traveling abroad.

More than a hundred years ago there was written a song that still has the power to bring a tear to those patriots who will really sit and listen to it. 'American the Beautiful' was written by Katherine Bates and in 1895 first published by The Congregationalist. Following 9-11, if you recall, Dan Rather quoted the last verse of the song and nearly burst into tears on air.

It's a great song, and maybe instead of being overly proud of the mistakes our country has made, or terribly embarrassed by our grand successes we can all unify and look at the verses for what they are. A message of hope.

Bates was living in the gilded age, but there were tragedies enough even in her time. True she was a Wellesley girl, but she writes in a time in which there have been horrible train wrecks, the Homestead Strike claimed American lives and left families thrown out into the street, Lizzie Borden had been brought to trial just the previous year, and not long before that was the Wounded Knee massacre.

Surely a woman living in such troubled times as these couldn't have been able to see the beauty in the country around her. And yet she does, with such piercing clarity that a century later we read her words and are taken in by the verse.

In the first verse, she relates the physical power that the country has. She wrote this taking a cross country train trip and was inspired by what she saw. And yet, she reminds us that the most beautiful part of the country is the brotherhood we share. The crown of all we have that is good.

The second speaks of pilgrims, but not those who landed on the rock, I think. Instead, these are the passionate pilgrims who make a way through the wilderness. The pioneers of action and social view who make plain the path we need to take. And the confirmation is in the self-control they must exercise because the path is not for personal gain or liberty, but the Liberty of all the nation's people.

Verse three reminds us of the heroes that prove their belief and faith in what the country was founded on. All races and all creeds have died for the causes of the nation and as the songs goes, if they love this country and love mercy more than their own life, then they are truly our most noble children.

And then the fourth. And this is the hardest I think, especially now, having suffered on our native soil, we have come out of our heady belief in our immortality, to see the reality of our fragility. We are no longer undimmed by human tears, and yet, this verse's integrity is intact.

The last verse begins, speaking about the patriot dream. That is the intangible thing, which goes beyond, as she says, and sees beyond the years. She talks of Hope.

And that is what makes us beautiful. What makes America Beautiful is that amazing ability we have to hope. She had it even in 1895 when there were trains exploding and people dying, and massacres, and crazy murders and she still sat on that train and was inspired by her nation, and by the people that dwell in it. She looked at all the squalor and filth and said, "ah, but look at what we could do." And she wrote verse that still strikes to the core of us.

We teach our children in school that the American flag is a symbol. That the colors stand for Courage, for Purity, and for Justice; that might not be quite right. The flag stands for the Hope of those things. The Flag doesn't promise that beneath its shadow you will, without a doubt, find those things. Instead, the Flag says, "Here are our hopes." When we are at our best this is what we endeavor to do. This is what we wish for our whole nation. These things above all else. These are the ideals we will fight for; these are the dreams we will instill it in our children, and our children's children.

This holiday I hope that no matter what our political affiliation, no matter whose man or woman is in the political offices, no matter what our varying stands on all of the turbulent issues at hand right now, we can all take a day to relive the Hope that Bates captures. No matter what you think of the country, put out a flag in pride for what it stands for. Raise it will all your heart behind it with the understanding that we can all stand together on Hope that someday, "beyond the years," we will look at cities that truly do gleam without corruption or pollution or selfishness and know that the time for our tears is over, and the time for Brotherhood has arrived.

Hope with me, and work for that hope, "from sea to shining sea."

Church and Drool

Public schools have long hidden behind the separation of church and state when it comes to matters of faith. Ever since they were started, Christian schools have been pledging that their students were steeped in religious studies integral to character development. It would seem to me however that, aside from the three R's, these two approaches to education still have much in common. I would say that there is a lack of support toward the schools' student's personal developments that binds them together in their misguided habits. Harsh words for the only options in our children's education?

All adolescents need faith. I say this not as a religious professional or a medical analyst, but as someone who has "been in the trenches" with teenage students of all shapes and sizes. Not to proselytize my own religion, I will say that all students need faith in something. It is important for every individual to realize and believe in something bigger than themselves and their perception. It is faith that allows us to seek out, and to remake ourselves into better and better creatures of this world.

I will also say that schools, public and private, have been basically robbing our children of faith by inches every year for the past few decades.

More and more places of worship have been expected to be responsible for children's faith development from early on. Where schools once taught moral value, the churches are being expected to take up the slack. Which would most likely work well if other organizations were not undermining their efforts. Responsibilities in a society are often shared and adapted as that society changes.

I won't get on the soapbox of every child's mad whirlwind life that consists of thousands of extracurricular activities a month, or the need that our children desperately have to simply be children. However, I will denounce schools and houses of worship for not collaborating enough when it comes to a simple joint effort like mutual event and activity scheduling.

Schools and churches should seek each other out early in the year and exchange schedules of major upcoming events so that they could be planned around or changed.

I can understand the logistics of planning around the schedules of thirty local churches would be a little insane. Though having some kind of exchange would at least keep church and schools informed.

Not only is it the responsibility of the school boards and church directors to communicate with each other, but it is also the responsibility of every coach, every choir director, and every Christian educator to do their best to make allowances for the other. Our children should never have to decide between exercising their faith and supporting their school. Each should support the other in the best interests of every student's development.

There is a gross misconception within the secular world of schools. It has materialized as I have seen coaches and teachers who refuse to make allowances for church events, yet they expect top performance from their students. How can a student, whose spirit is lost in confusion and despair, be expected to perform at their best? Coaches, teachers, and educational directors, I challenge you to affirm your students' commitment and loyalty to their God and their faith. It is a much harder thing to do than harassing the student, but it sows greater rewards for us all in the future.

Imagine yourself as an adolescent. Our youth are trying to find their way into adulthood in the midst of their daily activities, yet what message is being sent to our youth by these teachers, coaches and religious directors? Are they not saying to our students that you must be either for your school or for your God? One or the other? Are the prayers I hear in locker rooms before games nothing but a front or a ploy to invoke the Almighty for a win? Doesn't religion speak about reaching out to all others in love?

I say take responsibility for the prayers you utter! Take responsibility for those students who are within your care!

When we, as adults, take on any role as a leader in the eyes of these youths, we are not simply there to instruct them to win, or sing well, or learn by rote. We are taking on a promise to that student that we will lead and direct them. An agreement saying that we have gone ahead and will show them the path along which a healthy and fulfilling adult life lie. It is the noblest cause to take on when you first look at students in the role of leader or teacher, but it is a cause that all of us must be prepared to face each day as they look to us for leadership, not just in a chosen field, but in their lives as well.

We now live in a world that has mothers and fathers working until 5:00 or so, and our kids are out of school around 3:00; there are two hours of non-supervised time in which we must be able to trust our librarians, our coaches, our church workers and our neighbors. Our society has changed and demands that we change with it.

What this means is that we have hidden behind the separation of church and state at the expense of our students and children's development. I've seen coaches berate players for wanting to attend faith retreat weekends and have seen youth directors roll their eyes when students miss activities and studies because of practice.

Persecution from church and schools must be laid to rest. Neither institution can expect the young people of this world to choose between the educational success and the moral and spiritual success of their lives. Both are equally important in developing whole, prepared adults.

Both sides must begin to work together to ensure that our young people are growing into decent people. Everything is at stake. Our children and youth are not only our future, but they are also our present and our guarantee that human beings may continue as a noble aspect of creation.

A Quiet Place

Isaiah 40:25-31(NIV)
*"To whom will you compare me?
Or who is my equal?" says the Holy One.
Lift your eyes and look to the heavens:
Who created all these? He who brings out the starry host one
by one and calls them each by name.
Because of his great power and mighty strength, not one of
them is missing.
Why do you say, O Jacob,
and complain, O Israel,
"My way is hidden from the LORD;
my cause is disregarded by my God"?
Do you not know?
Have you not heard?
The LORD is the everlasting God,
the Creator of the ends of the earth.
He will not grow tired or weary,
and his understanding no one can fathom.
He gives strength to the weary
and increases the power of the weak.
Even youths grow tired and weary,
and young men stumble and fall;
but those who hope in the LORD
will renew their strength.
They will soar on wings like eagles;
they will run and not grow weary,
they will walk and not be faint.*

Mark 1:35-39 (NIV)
Very early in the morning, while it was still dark, Jesus got up, left the house and went off to a solitary place, where he prayed. Simon and his companions went to look for him, and when they found him, they exclaimed: "Everyone is looking for you!"

Jesus replied, "Let us go somewhere else to the nearby villages so I can preach there also. That is why I have come."

So he traveled throughout Galilee, preaching in their synagogues and driving out demons.

Growing up, one of my favorite pastimes was to go stargazing. My dad shared his love of stars with my brother and me, and through him, the love was ushered to us. Ever the scholar, my dad didn't just have us looking at the stars and planets but was relating to us the size of the objects relative to earth. That struck a nerve with me early on. There was just something wonderful and mysterious about looking at an object so distant and so large in real time. We would take the telescope out into the yard and see the moons of Jupiter. On clear nights we could even see the smudge on Jupiter that was an Earth sized storm- -raging ever since humans had been looking at it. We spent nights trying to find and focus on the rings of Saturn, the phases of Venus, even the colorful brilliance of Orion's stars. In college, I continued the study and took Astronomy I as my science requirement and Astronomy II even when I had to cram it into an already full course-load.

Our passage from Isaiah reflects that beauty I know from years of looking up, as Jack Horkheimer always says: "Keep looking up!" God's majesty and artistic nature are communicated to us on a million different levels through the natural world. Even on inspirational greeting cards, we have captured pictures of starry nights, rushing streams, a burst of spring color. No matter if the source of the wonder is secular or non-secular, every person on this earth can agree on the spiritual power nature can have.

It should come then as no surprise, to witness in the gospel of Mark that Christ himself is equally moved by the sight of wonder. After days filled with people and preaching and healing, he gets up early, walks out of the house, and watches the sunrise.

There is a personality test that is the nation's standard in such tests. It's called the "Myers-Briggs" after the couple that first created it (if you haven't heard of it, you've probably seen it using the characters from Harry Potter or the MCU). It can nail you down pretty well and be pretty revealing and enlightening about things you didn't even know. I've taken it a few times as a part of Church leadership courses, or weekend retreats and for some reason my personality type is hard for some people to believe. Mostly because this gregarious loud persona hides an introvert.

Usually, people think of the extrovert as the one who is the social butterfly, out in the limelight, shaking hands, greeting the morning with a bright smile and spring in their step. While we picture the introverts and turtle-like cave dwellers who venture out at night and read by dim lamplights, shunning the laughter of crowds.

The truest definition of these two personality types, according to Myers-Briggs, however, is simple and far different. Introverts are merely those people who gain or regain their strength by being alone or doing more solitary things. Extroverts are those who gain strength by being out in crowds, surrounded by peers and friends.

I swear to you; I'm about as die hard an introvert as they get. I love being with people, going on week-long retreats, even parties. I routinely make my wife, Leah, go to gallery openings at the Green Hill Art Center even when her job there doesn't require that she attend, just because I love going. However, I can only exist doing these things for so long and afterwards I need time alone to recover. I love going on trips, especially with a crowd of people, but after a week at a Mission Camp, or something similar, I basically shut myself completely off from the world for a few days.

So, here too, we get a glimpse into the lifestyle of Jesus. Not just in this passage but in so many points in the Gospels we see that Jesus is very often doing his own thing. Going camping and fasting alone for 30 days, sleeping in the back of the boat, watching the sunrise alone, and even in his final hours he asks his closest friends to still pray a little way apart from Him.

This brings to light something for all of us, however. Whether, based on my hasty description, you see yourself as either an introvert or an extrovert, we must all benefit from time spent "refilling our tanks." Even Christ himself did not constantly run at 100% all the time, seven days a week. Even though he healed on the Sabbath he knew exactly what it meant to take a Sabbath moment. We can find him praying alone, being peaceful, waiting, allowing God the time and opportunity to dwell more closely. Even Christ, who was God incarnate, allowed time out of a ministry that was the most important in history and one that he knew was only going to last three years. He still carved out the time to be only with his Master and Creator.

Every person in the world has been weary. Every one of us has been weak when we most needed to be strong. Scripture states so truly and so rightly that even the young stumble and fall.

Yet, what does the Bible promise us? If we hope in the Lord, if we let everything ride on God if we cast every chance, we have at prosperity in this life on Him alone, then we will be renewed--made new again. Then it goes on, promising more than being new, we will soar! On wings like eagles. We will run and never tire.

But how? How do we hope in the Lord? What is the activity that does this thing? Many things, a life like Christ. We have here, one facet of instruction. Find that quiet place. Watch that sunrise.

That alone can be incredibly difficult. In the world of today we in the world of today, we can feel that there are so many different things pulling us in so many different directions. A moment of peace is all we can get and even then, that is asking a lot. My wife and I both have been incredibly blessed to have traveled to Italy. Unfortunately we went on separate trips. The other day we were reminiscing about our experiences and one of the things we both missed was busy restaurants.

Sounds like a crazy thing to miss from a couple of introverts, right? The thing is neither one of us was fluent in Italian. So, in the midst of 60 or 70 animated conversations, all we heard were the lyrical tones of a fairly beautiful language. Something like that is possible I think no matter where we are. By process of mind we can somehow turn off the part of our brain that is absorbing input from the world, let it fade into the white noise of life and find a kind of surreal peacefulness.

I wonder sometimes if Christ didn't do something exactly like this during the insane parts of his trial with the Sanhedrin in the last hours of his life. Shut them off, let them fade to the background, find peace, and talk with his Father.

In this piece of scripture, he has found peace in the colors God has laid out for him in the early morning. When Simon finally finds Jesus, apparently, he didn't leave a note before going out, they ask him, as any of us might as, "Where in the world have you been!? We've been looking for you all morning!" But Jesus gives his reply, and--did you catch this? -not even acknowledging their questions! Instead, the scripture says that Jesus replied, "Let us go somewhere else -- to the nearby villages -- so I can preach there also. That is why I have come." He tells them instead of His Purpose.

I can almost picture the scene. Simon is puffing up the side of the hill, and breathlessly asks:

'Oh, phew. Jesus. Where have you been? Man, we were, (gasp) looking everywhere for you. What are you doing?'

Jesus is still looking toward the sunrise and simply delivers to Simon and the others the instructions for the next few weeks. Can you hear the subtext in Jesus' words? we've heard them before: "Where have you been? We were looking for you!"

Comes Jesus answer, "I have been about my Father's business."

Like Christ, we must find our way to separate ourselves from the worries of the world. No note, no apologies, just communion with God. We cannot expect ourselves to function without finding those places in life where we feel able to commune with the Almighty. Whether it is a sunrise, a sunset, a gloriously refurbished sanctuary, or a just a step outside on the porch. It doesn't have to belong--it doesn have to be an hour or thirty days--it just has to happen.

The promise of renewal, of energy, of flight that is fancy-free is there. Waiting for those who can find that quiet place in the physical realm, or in the mental and spiritual one, but a place that is apart from the world long enough for God to bring solace and instruction on the next piece of our journey.

Builders

Matthew 7:21-29 (CEV)
Not everyone who calls me their Lord will get into the kingdom of heaven. Only the ones who obey my Father in heaven will get in. On the day of judgment many will call me their Lord.

They will say, "We preached in your name, and in your name, we forced out demons and worked many miracles." But I will tell them, "I will have nothing to do with you! Get out of my sight, you evil people!"

Anyone who hears and obeys these teachings of mine is like a wise person who built a house on solid rock. Rain poured down, rivers flooded, and winds beat against that house. But it did not fall, because it was built on solid rock.

Anyone who hears my teachings and doesn't obey them is like a foolish person who built a house on sand. The rain poured down, the rivers flooded, and the winds blew and beat against that house. Finally, it fell with a crash.

When Jesus finished speaking, the crowds were surprised at his teaching. He taught them like someone with authority, and not like their teachers of the Law of Moses.

When I was in Mexico on a mission trip, a song by the group "Big Tent Revival" kept playing in my head. It's called 'Two Sets of Jones' and it basically chronicles the lives of two married couples. One, who is wealthy and depends on their material goods to get them through life, and the other, who have "nothing but Jesus," and can only depend on Him for their daily needs. Sadly, as you can probably guess the marriage without Christ fails and ends in a bitter divorce.

The chorus is great though: And the rain came down, and it blew the four walls down, and the clouds they rolled away, one set of Jones' was standing that day.

At first, it was for the fact that it seemed everything in the neighborhoods we worked in was built on the sandy soil. I was amazed, and thought, how do they keep their houses from washing away? I learned later that they didn't and there was a local push to teach the Mexicans who were moving into the cities and shanty towns how to adequately build.

In the second place, this song was in my head because we were there with so many of our church's young people, from the earliest days of high school to a few who were in college. And I kept thinking how like this verse we all were. I could see some of them who were building on the solid rock, some who wanted to build on the sand, others who had built on sand and were now dealing with the great collapse.

Yet, could I blame those who built on sand? It's hard to build on solid ground. Any builder worth his salt knows that you have to dig down to set the foundation of any building. That topsoil of any nature is liable to shift without warning and cause defects in the structure.

This is one reason why Jesus uses this illustration--he is after all a true-blue collar worker, a man whose life was spent not wholly in the synagogue but in the workshop learning both his earthly and heavenly Fathers' trades.

I've been on habitat house projects and the thing about digging a foundation is that--it's really hard work. I mean you talk about ditch digging and I'll tell you, they put a shovel in my hands. And we got right to work, and I mean on the very first day. I met the family whose house this would be, and we began digging. There is no heavier shovelful than that first one. You look out over the surveyor's lines and you see the amount of work left to be done. You get overwhelmed before the first blister even surfaces. Digging a foundation is tough. So how could I really blame these young people, who without whatever direction they needed in their lives had gone on their own chosen the path of least resistance? It is a simple thing to go to church with Mom and Dad while growing up, there are no Christian police to check up and ensure you are following God's Law.

In college, we once joked about the "God Squad" who would come to the dorm rooms of offenders, break down the door, and attack without mercy, bludgeoning you with a rubber fish. That's an ichthus reference.

But there is no such group in real life. It is a simple and easy thing for us to pay lip service to Christ and act in a way that is easiest for us. This, we know, has never been enough for Christ. In the book of Revelation, He warns of the lukewarm, saying that he will vomit the lukewarm believers out of His mouth.

Yet, Jesus knew how much work it was to set your house on a firm stone. He uses this metaphor to tell the people not only what the wise will do, but also what he expects from u--hard work. But great is the reward. Your house will weather the storms of life. Listen closely though to Christ's warning in this: Yes, we are fully redeemed by grace and His blood, but this act only opens the door for us to make the choice. Will our lives be that reflection of His teachings, or when we reach the gates, will we then be surprised for Jesus to look at us and say--" I'm sorry who are you again?"

To paraphrase the verse we are looking at here, not everyone who calls me Lord will get into the kingdom of heaven.

I know many of those people. Those who claimed God with their lips but betrayed him with their actions. "But Lord, we did many things in your name!" Comes the mighty answer,

"Get out of my sight!" He calls those "evil people."

What we do is important. Our lives must be filled with two-fold purpose. Not only must we act--our faith must have works else it is called dead. But, we must, in addition, do it in faith in the name of the one who sends us.

Before we went south of the border, we had many orientation dates; teaching everyone young and old how to better "come in the name of Christ." Don't snub food, be kind in spite of everything, and remember they give us the best of what they have.

It is a simple thing to show up anywhere with a t-shirt that had the cross on it, it's infinitely more difficult to change your actions--more so being in a harsh and different environment. Honestly, even though our accommodations were adequate while we stayed there in Mexico it was hard--for some this was their first trip away from home. But there has to come a point in life when we must leave the house our parents have built for us and decide where to build our own.

In the converse studying my young friends, and as a warning, it is never too late to have your house washed away, or to find new wisdom with which to build it again.

Here's another scenario: there was a house in rural West Virginia that was slowly slipping into a ravine. The foundation was cracked and failing. Here was a home that was at one time built on solid ground, but the only choice we had was to tear it down and build again.

Being in Habitat for Humanity taught me a lot. A firm foundation requires two basic things. Firm ground and sturdy materials. Either one without the other and the house is doomed to fall. Good deeds are not enough. The simple name of Christ is not enough. Both must be worked together to create a secure and sturdy dwelling.

The magical thing about a Habitat house is the other people working on it. The trench I dug would have taken me six months to get right doing it alone. I vividly remember looking out at the surveyor's lines and feeling desperate. "We will never get this done. It's impossible." And after the first full day of digging I thought about giving up, asking our leaders to switch to a different work team for the rest of the week. Yet, I pressed on and with the right leadership and other willing hands we had it done that next day.

I was able to finish the foundation of my first house with Habitat because I came to rely on the people around me who knew how to hold a shovel, what gloves to wear, how to switch grips and give one group of muscles a rest, how to keep true to the surveyor's line.

Let the body of believers hold you up and place a deep and firm foundation within you. Let us rely on one another for the sturdiness in our lives which will then weather any storm that life can place upon us. In a way, we are that God Squad and though we may not attack with rubber fish, we may show up on a doorstep with a casserole and an open ear.

Let the rivers flood, let life cast out onto us what it will, because I know my life to be built on solid rock. And though my basement may flood, the shutter may bang in the wind and my roof may drip from time to time, these things can be repaired if I rely on those whom God has provided, and I know that the foundation of the house will stand fast and strong.

Further, we as the church are the foundation upon which the House of God is built, and Christ can be the indestructible rock upon which all things can rest. Without one or the other, the House will crumble into dust.

Be the Judge

Exodus 14:19-31 (NRSV)
Then the angel of God who was going before the host of Israel moved and went behind them, and the pillar of cloud moved from before them and stood behind them, coming between the host of Egypt and the host of Israel. And there was the cloud and the darkness. And it lit up the night[a] without one coming near the other all night.

Then Moses stretched out his hand over the sea, and the LORD drove the sea back by a strong east wind all night and made the sea dry land, and the waters were divided. And the people of Israel went into the midst of the sea on dry ground, the waters being a wall to them on their right hand and on their left. The Egyptians pursued and went in after them into the midst of the sea, all Pharaoh's horses, his chariots, and his horsemen. And in the morning watch the LORD in the pillar of fire and of cloud looked down on the Egyptian forces and threw the Egyptian forces into a panic, clogging their chariot wheels so that they drove heavily. And the Egyptians said, "Let us flee from before Israel, for the LORD fights for them against the Egyptians."

Then the LORD said to Moses, "Stretch out your hand over the sea, that the water may come back upon the Egyptians, upon their chariots, and upon their horsemen." So Moses stretched out his hand over the sea, and the sea returned to its normal course when the morning appeared. And as the Egyptians fled into it; the LORD threw[c] the Egyptians into the midst of the sea. The waters returned and covered the chariots and the horsemen; of all the host of Pharaoh that had followed them into the sea, not one of them remained. But the people of Israel walked on dry ground through the sea, the waters being a wall to them on their right hand and on their left.

Thus the LORD saved Israel that day from the hand of the Egyptians, and Israel saw the Egyptians dead on the seashore.

Israel saw the great power that the LORD used against the Egyptians, so the people feared the LORD, and they believed
in the LORD and in his servant Moses.

Romans 14:1-12 (NRSV)

As for the one who is weak in faith, welcome him, but not to quarrel over opinions. One person believes he may eat anything, while the weak person eats only vegetables. Let not
the one who eats despise the one who abstains and let not the one who abstains pass judgment on the one who eats, for God has welcomed him.

Who are you to pass judgment on the servant of another? It is before his own master that he stands or falls. And he will be upheld, for the Lord is able to make him stand.

One person esteems one day as better than another, while another esteems all days alike. Each one should be fully convinced in his own mind. The one who observes the day, observes it in honor of the Lord. The one who eats, eats in honor of the Lord, since he gives thanks to God, while the one who abstains, abstains in honor of the Lord and gives thanks to God. For none of us lives to himself, and none of us dies to
himself. If we live, we live to the Lord, and if we die, we die to the Lord. So then, whether we live or whether we die, we are the Lord's. For to this end Christ died and lived again, that he might be Lord both of the dead and of the living.

Why do you pass judgment on your brother? Or you, why do you despise your brother? For we will all stand before the judgment seat of God; for it is written, "As I live, says the Lord, every knee shall bow to me, and every tongue shall confess to God."

So then each of us will give an account of himself to God.

When I was in college, a favorite pastime of my friends and I was to challenge each other in coming up with the very best jabs for one another. One such time, my roommate made a comment to another friend, and before I could stop myself, I said,'That's not funny Now, not in a reprimand mind you, but instead in the voice of total authority. My roommate turned to me and questioned, "What are you, the Judge of Funny?" Thus for many months afterwards I was dubbed "the Judge of

Funny," and if any joke was uttered in my presence, my friends would stop and say, "Wait, wait, don't anybody laugh--we'd better clear this with Chris first." It was a friendly poke at my expense and good-natured. But it was revealing. It showed a side of myself I can still feel poking out every once in a while, even now. I'm the judge.

I don't know if it was because of my being the first born, or some deep sense of justice my mother passed on to me, but my whole life, I have struggled not to pass judgment, or at the very least not express my feelings on it.

In another example, I will relate a story my Dad is often fond of recalling. Dad is a teacher of gifted students in the county where we grew up. I was in several of his classes, but one of the first, when I was in fifth grade, was an elementary physics class. Our first project in our first class was a group challenge. Two groups pitted against each other in a race to balance a broom on the top of a chair. We were given no further instruction or hints and were given creative reign to solve the problem as best as we saw fit. I had the benefit of learning about an object's balance point earlier in life with Dad in some random summer afternoon, and, recalling that, saw that this was much the same exercise. After listening to some of my other peers· solutions, which were not working, I finally lost all patience, snatched the broom out of a girl's hand, laid it on top of the chair, balanced it perfectly, and shouted at her, "All you have to do is find the center of gravity." Well, she burst into tears, and Dad immediately called me into the hallway. Not to detail my punishment but suffice to say that neither my brother nor I ever found favoritism in dad's classes. I had judged this girl and found her wanting and doled out her retribution. Dad always said she never recovered and is probably living in some commune in Wyoming trying to find inner peace.

It can be hard not to judge people. My defence to my Dad in the hallway was something to the effect of, "But they were wrong!" It seemed unfair that I should suffer for getting it right.

Well to that let's take a look at the teachings of Paul to the Romans. In this letter, he takes care to outline instructions for everyday life; instructions that lead to wholeness of not only the faith community but also of the individual. He is writing, not only for the Jewish believer converted out of the idea that Jesus is the prophesied Messiah, but also to the group of Gentiles that reside there. To them, Jesus is a completely new and radical way of thinking. They are taking the leap not from Hope in Prophecy to Prophecy Fulfillment, but the leap from a myriad of gods and goddesses to the belief in the One true Creator and the path to Life through a man who was that Deity's Son--Love Incarnate on Earth. Of course, Paul is also dealing with two very distinct groups of people who are having trouble getting along.

Poor Paul. He's trying to bring them eternal, everlasting spiritual truth and they are arguing over dietary nuances. For the Jews, their way of life is truly changing in the light of Jesus' teachings. Through Paul's interpretation through the word and the Spirit he sees, and rightfully so, that Jesus as Messiah is for the whole world, not just the Jews. He is the fulfillment not only of prophecy but also with the greater promise spoken first to Adam and to every living human on the planet. Which is: 'I love you. I want us to be together

The Jews of Rome are dealing with judgment.

For so long they have been accustomed to being God's chosen people. His only chosen. He chose them to inhabit Israel, above all the others who were already living there. He chose them to carry his promise, above all the others who dwelt in the Fertile Crescent. He chose them to come out of Egypt, above all the other nations that had been made slaves by that empire. And now, suddenly, the Day of Glory has come« but it has come for all people and all nations.

Talk about your big let downs.

Suddenly, God doesn't have favorites. He has redeemed all by the blood. Paul sites several things in the passage. One of the first is his question to the Christians of Rome, "Has God not owned all those who profess belief in Him and in Christ? Then who are we, to disown them? To do so, to pass judgment on people, is to usurp the place of God." He also warns against the feelings between the strong and the weak. Again, we have divisions in the early church, not only between Gentile and Jew but also between those who are strong and secure in the faith and those who are new and weak. Judgment can come out in so many ways. Condescension is one of the most often used tools of Judgment.

But it is hard not to judge.

I can feel for the Jews. After millennia of being the teacher's pet in every way, they suddenly have to give that up. They are just like everyone else. And even if they attain a solid faith -- what is their reward? Sameness. There is no hierarchy in the Kingdom of Heaven.

In the Methodist church I grew up in, they have conference Bishops who are elected by the ministerial body and rule over the general sessions. I was amazed at one General Assembly in which the bishop came down from the dais and washed the feet of my friends and I who were attending. My pastor, who was with us, saw me and said simply, "We are all believers, struggling to come closer to God." The words of the Disciples to Christ rang out, "No teacher, surely you will not wash our feet. It is only our human perception that creates the feudal system of believers.

Paul reminds the Jews especially of god's words from Isaiah, a book they more than likely knew very well. Chapter 45:23 says "Every knee will bow before me." He says to them in this letter. Just before that in Isaiah 45: 22, God speaks of "the Ends of the Earth" turning towards Him to be saved. Paul reminds them that even in the prophecy, God addresses every nation when it comes to salvation.

In re-reading the Exodus passage from the Old Testament, I was reminded of a wonderfully epic theatre experience that I was treated to in the movie "The Prince of Egypt." You can sometimes do in a cartoon what your budget will not allow you to do in live action. Moses, upon God's command, stretches out his hand and the water roll back in an awesome display. Dolphins and fish can be seen silhouetted in the water as the nation walks by them.

In scripture, however, we must imagine something more than even that. Not only did the waters rollback, but a powerful wind came and dried the land that was at the bottom of the sea.

In addition, look at the chronology of the miracle. Moses with God's power allows some of the water to come back on and destroy the Egyptian chariots. While the nation is still in the trough with them. Yet they continue, unfettered. At the end of the verse we are blessed by the understatement, "Israel saw the great power of the Lord, so they were in awe of Him and believed."

This is what it takes to be the judge. This kind of might, this kind of mind-boggling power. Do you have what it takes to fulfill the role of God as a judge? I surely do not.

So then, we are called and commanded to not pass judgment on our brothers and sisters in Christ, who are all people. We can use the verse from Isaiah as a mantra if we must: "Every knee will bow, every tongue confesses."

What then is the action verb to go along with this omission in behavior? After this verse, Paul immediately goes on in Romans with a resolution: "Make up your mind not to be a stumbling block." This is the active opposite of not judging. In this, he asks us to not place anything in the path of those who are trying to come to the Lord: to resolute ourselves to not create an obstacle course to the loving arms of God. There is still more to it, however.

Recently, a friend of mine was letting me in on a little piece of farm lore concerning cows. If cows are looking down and there is anything in their way, they will stop. Be it a body, a car, or a twig they are immovable. So, with that in mind, I'll paint you a scenario, a parable.

It's a bitter winter and the cattle need to spend the night in the barn. The father entrusts his son and his daughter to put them there. Now, they put out fresh hay, open the doors, and see the cows within sight of the barn coming toward it. The next morning the cows are all dead. Bringing the two children out to dead animals the farmer shows them a branch that was in their path to the barn. Being cows, they had stopped and frozen to death. The boy is indignant and says, "But father, we didn't put that branch there!" And on the way to the woodshed to discipline the children, the father replies, "But neither did you remove it."

Paul's real objective in all this is to build a more perfect Christian community. Not being a stumbling block is not only to not become a detriment to someone else's spiritual life but also, in the flipside, to do everything in our power to better it. In verse nineteen of the same chapter, Paul charges the church to make every effort to do what is mutually upbuilding of one another.

I've heard that to repent means to make an about-face from a sin or wrongdoing and face God. The repentant opposite then of Judgment is this mutual up-building that Paul is talking about.

As I said, it's tough. It's hard not to judge. We must all be ever vigilant to turn away from those self-righteous temptations and instead reach lovingly out to those weaker in the faith and bring one another into a place of mutual strengthening.

It's this that makes the Church and our faith strong. It's this that allows the church to grow in love and rightness toward God.

Judgment not only demeans the ones we judge but falsely elevates the judge to a position so lofty we cannot hope to keep up with the image it creates. We are doomed to tarnish it. Better then to leave the judging to the untarnishable, and to instead, focus our efforts on being honest about our own shortcomings and aiding one another in overcoming them for the larger glory of Christ on earth.

The Cost of Christ

Mark 8:31-38 (NRSV)
He then began to teach them that the Son of Man must suffer many things and be rejected by the elders, chief priests and teachers of the law, and that he must be killed and after three days rise again. He spoke plainly about this, and Peter took him aside and began to rebuke him.

But when Jesus turned and looked at his disciples, he rebuked Peter. "Get behind me, Satan!" he said. "You do not have in mind the things of God, but the things of men."

Then he called the crowd to him along with his disciples and said:

"If anyone would come after me, he must deny himself and take up his cross and follow me. For whoever wants to save his life will lose it, but whoever loses his life for me and for the gospel will save it.

What good is it for a man to gain the whole world, yet forfeit is soul? Or what can a man give in exchange for his soul? If anyone is ashamed of me and my words in this adulterous and sinful generation, the Son of Man will be ashamed of him when he comes in his Father's glory with the holy angels."

Jesus asks a lot of us.

Yet, there are those who work tirelessly for the cause of Christ. If you look you can find evidence of their work in many of life's facets -- large and small. When people act well and work hard in the name of Chris it is, in some way, like putting out the best set of china and silver for beloved guests. Nothing is thought of except the blessing the host can give to those who are coming.

During an Ash Wednesday service at my church we read Jesus· instructions for fasting and prayer. Reminders that these disciplines are sacred things between us and God alone, which truly must be against our human desires. When we do something good, we want, what my wife and I call, "pets and scratches."

When we were newly married, my wife received, as a gift, a book called "The Five Love Languages," by Gary Chapman. In this book we discovered that my love language or the way in which I understand that someone loves me, is from the recognition of my work. I forget how "pets and scratches" started but it became a half joke. If I was mentioning some maintenance items that I had done more than a few times, my wife, Leah, knew I felt like I had missed out on "pets and scratches" or full recognition of my work. Barring the fact that a little bit of recognition is healthy and nice, how are people like me supposed to reconcile ourselves to the work of Christ? Which often is meant, is intentioned, to go unnoticed, except by God? Well, we are supposed to get by partly from depending on faith in His blessings, and the rest from practiced patience. Even still--that's asking a lot don't you think?

In verse 34, Jesus lays it all flat out for the disciples and basically anyone in earshot who he has gathered around him. "If you want to follow me, your life is forfeit." I love the fishermen disciples--Peter and Andrew and the others. In some way, I feel like I identify better with them than with the tax collector or any of the rest. I feel like I could in some way know what was going on in their brains at different points when Jesus reveals certain things to them. We forget sometimes how astounded they must have been at certain times! For instance, I've seen all six episodes of the Star Wars movies. The story is very involved in some places and having seen it so many times I forget the "big reveals" of the story and how they appear to first timers. Think back to the very first time you realized Darth Vader (warning spoilers!) was Luke's father. Watch it with someone seeing it for the first time, and they are filled with shock and disbelief.

Knowing how scripture turns out is a little like that. I think we forget that when Jesus begins talking to his friends of many years about his impending torture and demise at the hands of the Sanhedrin they are floored and depressed, to say the least! Add to that his promise that he would be raised from the dead. So many things about Christ's true purpose were missed by the Disciples. They had seen him raise Lazarus, sure, but who will do the raising when he is in the tomb himself? Earlier in this same chapter, in verse 21, he reminds them of the miracle of the loaves and fish, of the abundance created out of even a small gift. Yet they are still fretting over food and trivial things. Jesus comment with frustration: "Why do you not yet understand?"

Jesus is asking a lot out of the Disciples. Peter, poor Peter, tries to get Jesus aside for a moment, perhaps to talk some sense into the guy scaring everybody with stories of death. I have a fiction book written about the life of Christ that is basically a paraphrase on the Gospel. It's a fun read and lends itself well to create a very human experience. Yet, one of my favorite moments is when Jesus gives Simon a nickname. In the Bible, it usually reads Simon, who is also called Peter, or something near to that in every translation. In the novel it comes up in

one of these, "Why are you folks not getting this?" moments that Jesus frequently has, in which he cries, "Simon, you got a mind like a rock." I love being able to think that Jesus created this good-natured jibe and the apostles picked it up. I think I love it so much because I could see Christ saying the same thing about me.

But dear Simon-Peter, in this instance, is made an example of. We're getting down to the wire of the ministry and I imagine Christ could have been a little anxious with the disciples to finally grasp some of what has been going on. So he shouts, "Your thoughts are not from God, but from men!"

Imagine what Peter could have said to him« Probably the exact same thing any of us would say if a dear friend and traveling companion told us that they were going to die.

"No, no, Jesus don't say these things. You know how James gets--he's very emotional. I think you are scaring him. Look, why don't we skirt Jerusalem for a while, until after Passover, we'll go back to Capernaum, you can do some preaching there, we'll take some time off. Look it will be ok. All right? No one has to die. Listen to reason."

Those can all be loving, loving words. Nothing wrong with them. But we must be wary. Good is not Godly. Kindness is not the Kingdom. Works alone don't get us into heaven. When Jesus rebukes Peter, I think we tend to imagine that his words must have been so terrible to have Jesus react so. But in truth, Jesus was reacting to the deceiver who was using Peter's words to speak to Jesus. The subtext of Christ's words here are Oh Peter, dear friends: How much I wish I could go with you to Capernaum. How I long to be on a fishing boat with you instead of before Caiaphas. How wonderful it would be to watch you raise families, continue this ministry and watch it grow. But Christ knows.

He asks nothing of us that He himself is not already doing. He knows the Father's will and the scenes that must play out. He repeats to the Disciples the words he hears from God his own Father. If you want to be mine, then your whole life is mine.

When we read that we must give up desires, we imagine the vices, the selfish things we all do. And that's true. It also means giving up good intentions. We think that we must do right instead of wrong when in actuality, we must understand that we must do only what God perceives as right, which in our eyes, and in the eyes of the world, may appear so very wrong.

Look again to our example in scripture. It is madness by all the standards of the time for Christ to go to the one hotspot where he is sure to be recognized and acted upon. So much earlier in the gospels do we read that the Sanhedrin begins to plot against Jesus. They have not been idle all that time, and the Disciples know it! By the world's standards and by logical conclusion what Jesus was doing was madness. Though, it was the true course in God's plan. What Peter said to Christ was probably very loving and kind, but in the sight of God, it was a temptation against the will of God.

So, in this season of Lent, in this time of penitence (which is simply expressing remorse for our sins), instead of struggling to identify the bad things and do good, we are set free by Christ's words. Free to identify that which is Godly, and joyfully do the things which the world might find crazy, but which bring a smile to the heart of God. Jesus pointedly says, perhaps to Simon, "the Rock," as much as to anyone else in verse 36. I could do the right thing, Peter, the thing that seems like justice and the logical thing to do, or I can do the will of my Father.

This season of Lent is one of reflection, and one of action, not of good deeds, but of Godly ones--those done in joy and out of love for God and God alone.

Dusty Teva's

Mark 6:1-13 (CEV)
Jesus left and returned to his hometown with his disciples. The next Sabbath he taught in the Jewish meeting place.

Many of the people who heard him were amazed and asked, "How can he do all this? Where did he get such wisdom and the power to work these miracles? Isn't he the carpenter, the son of Mary? Aren't James, Joseph, Judas, and Simon his brothers? Don't his sisters still live here in our town?"

The people were very unhappy because of what he was doing. But Jesus said, "Prophets are honored by everyone, except the people of their hometown and their relatives and their own family."

Jesus could not work any miracles there, except to heal a few sick people by placing his hands on them. He was surprised that the people did not have any faith.

Then Jesus went around teaching from village to village. Calling the Twelve to him, he sent them out two by two and gave them authority over evil[b] spirits.

These were his instructions: "Take nothing for the journey except a staff -- no bread, no bag, no money in your belts.

Wear sandals but not an extra tunic. Whenever you enter a house, stay there until you leave that town. And if any place will not welcome you or listen to you, shake the dust off your feet when you leave, as a testimony against them."

They went out and preached that people should repent. They drove out many demons and anointed many sick people with oil and healed them.

Let's start out with a fairytale. I think we all know the story of Peter Pan, but it's not so much the boy who would never grow up that I want to focus on, instead, let's turn our attention to the folklore surrounding his faithful compatriot: Tinkerbell.

As you might know, she was a fairy, tiny bug wings, magic dust and all the rest. When I was young there was a particular part of the story that always worried me about her though. The lore says that fairies were born when the first baby gave its first laugh and the laugh broke into a million pieces. And each piece became a fairy. But every time someone said they didn't believe, then a fairy somewhere would drop out of the sky! When I was young, I was so profoundly vexed by this idea because it was something that was making the leap from the story world into my own. I had real power over the fairies in another land! They depended on me! I was very careful never to say that I didn't believe.

Oddly this was the first thing that came into my head when I was reading the passage from Mark. The first part actually, wherein Jesus is preaching in his hometown, which understandably is hard to do, but zero-in on the last few verses of that story verses 5 and 6, in which it is saying that he was unable to do any real miracles there, because of their lack of faith.

Now, I am in no way comparing fable and fact--between Christ and the world of Peter Pan. However, the thread remains that we do have power, in a fashion, over the miracles of Christ.

I have two things I want us to think about out of these two stories from Mark and this is the first: Christ depends on us. The second being that he equips us, but more on that later.

Now, the Almighty does not depend on us at all in the same way little Tinkerbell does. Go back to the scriptures, we already know that they are in a mood of disbelief all throughout his teaching in the synagogue, afterwards, Jesus says that they have treated him without honor, and aside from healing the sick, he was unable to do miracles there, and then Jesus is amazed at their lack of faith.

What this verse does is lay the responsibility of the work of Jesus Christ firmly on our doorstep. There is a familiar painting that I'm sure many of you have seen of Christ standing at the door knocking. Standing outside in a garden, and dressed in his usual raiment he leans in, staff in the opposite hand, and is tapping on the door. It's a very sweet picture and seemingly without a deeper message until you realize one thing about the painting. There is no doorknob on the door. The door can only be opened from the inside. So with certainty we all know that it is we who hold the power of letting Christ into our hearts, there to dwell3 however, through this verse from Mark, and Christ's own actions, we are brought deeper into the understanding of what it is to let Christ in. We can let him first to our hearts, we can meet him in the doorway to aide him in doing his work, or we can slam the door coldly in his face. Just as the people of his hometown did. And so, he was helpless to aide them. Moreover he was amazed! You'd think as God's son it would take a lot really amaze Jesus. Well, this does it. He is healing the sick before them, bringing the word of God to their ears--can you imagine what it was like to hear Jesus himself preach?! Yet, he is met with a total lack of faith.

Taking this knowledge though, that our faith, and our belief and utter trust in Christ is integral to his success in ministry, if we take that as our lens and look to other verses in the Bible, we can see another layer to Christ's words.

Look up Matthew 23:13, where Jesus says woe to the Scribes and Pharisees for leading people in the wrong way; in Romans 14:13 Paul preaches against us putting stumbling blocks in the path of our fellow believers; again, in the first letter to John 2:10, he talks of how those believers that love their brothers and sisters in Christ will dwell in the light.

This last verse puts it most succinctly: we live righteous lives, not for our own sake, but out of love for other believers. This is a whole new way of thinking really. Live in God's will and in Faith, not for your own sake, but so that Jesus can do true miracles for other people. Our belief and righteous living are then important to the overall ministry of Christ, and it is that ministry that we are betraying when we act outside the will of God, not just our own little corner. That's a pretty big responsibility.

As is His usual method, Jesus does not leave us ill-equipped to handle this. The very next part of the gospel gives us instruction.

When Jesus sends out the Twelve Apostles there is a section where it sounds like he is taking the time to give them some fashion tips for reaching the faithless. To really get what he was saying here, I am going to have to briefly lead us through what the average Jewish man wore on a daily basis.

There are actually five different pieces that they wore. The first (1) was called the chiton, which was the most basic piece. Think of a long sack with holes cut in it for the head and arms. That was it. The next piece (2) was the himation. This is what the movies pieced up on; it's a giant piece of cloth that is wrapped around the waist and over the shoulder. The third (3) is a simple girdle, or belt; a long piece of cloth about two spans wide that you could fold in the middle so you could keep your money in it. The fourth (4) was a headdress 2 not quite the Arab keffiyeh, but close. A big square piece that was folded diagonally, the folded part goes across your brow. And lastly, (5) a pair of sandals.

So what does Jesus have them take? A staff, sandals, and the tunic. Not even an extra tunic. Not even money.

I tell you; I would think that Jesus had some planning issues. I'm kind of a type "A" personality when it comes to planning a mission trip and when we go out, I have two or three giant Tupperware© tubs that I take. Jesus sounds like he is sending these guys out grossly under-prepared if you ask me.

Let's look at the context of this verse. Where in the story of his ministry are we? Somewhere near the middle, maybe. This might be what you call a practice run for the twelve. Already Jesus is preparing them for life without him. And to that end, he is also using this excursion as a time to preach repentance, but also as a time to teach the apostles what being his follower means. It's hard for us to remember sometimes that Jesus is starting from the ground up with these guys.

The disciples were to live in utter humility and simplicity. Take a staff, because you got a long road to haul ahead of you. He then says, 'take no wallet, or money '--now the reason here could be twofold. First, it was a well-known rabbinic law of the time that when you entered the temple you would take off your shoes and set aside your money belt or wallet. The idea was that all ordinary things were to be set aside. It could be that here Christ is saying that the homes there were to enter were every bit as sacred as the Temple courts, or that their entire ministry would be out of the ordinary. Second, there were Pharisees who would travel from town to town collecting in their wallets for the synagogues of that area, perhaps Christ also wanted to ensure that people knew they were coming only with the word of God, and not also with a handout for their dutiful offering.

There were to wear sandals, again, this is not a pleasure cruise. You will be hiking it out there. And no extra garments, which could be perceived as extravagant and wasteful living. So here we have the follower of Christ as he himself would have it: pared down to utter simplicity, complete trust, and a generosity that is out to give and never demand. Keep in mind, though, that this was a short-term ministry, not Christ's rules for living the rest of their lives.

So then, when we are about the work of the church, how must we prepare ourselves?

There is a passage in a Roman novel called 'Qu Vadis It talks about a young Roman who has fallen for a Christian girl. Though because he is not a Christian, she will have nothing to do with him. To find out what Christians are all about he follows her to a meeting one night and listens to Peter preaching from outside the house. As he listens something happens to him and he later thinks that, "if he wished to follow that teaching he would have to place all his thoughts, his habits, his character, and his whole nature up to that moment on a burning pyre, and fill himself up with an altogether different and entirely new soul."

That newness is what we seek, but what is the cost? The Roman boy had it right. Everything that we have essentially needs to be tossed out. What Jesus asked the Twelve to do was very much an entirely new thing. Go out without all those other pieces of clothing on? They would have felt naked! Taking no bread! Relying on others for their very sustenance? Take no money?!

What Jesus asks of them is a radical reconfiguring of their ideas on how to reach people with the word of God. And there was much they would have to throw on the burning pyre in order to do it.

What is the outcome of dressing for ministry in the way Christ asks? What happens when we open the door to Christ wide, into our hearts and also wholly into His work?

What happened to David--who was called the Beloved of God? In Samuel, you can read that David. as the newly anointed king, proceeds to take back Zion and rule there for thirty-three years. The verse reads that "he became more and more powerful because the Lord Almighty was with him."

Exist in the power of the Lord and blessings will be yours. For David those blessings were in the form of the power of a ruler. As for the people of Jesus· hometown? What would their blessings have been if they had faith? As it was Jesus healed the sick!

That's the other way this works. If we are in God's presence, then we will have blessings. But, if our faith is lacking, if we do not have the door wide open, then the full blessings will not be ours! The full measure heaped up and running over! That is the blessing of someone who is able to set self aside for the sake of God's ministry. That is the blessing of someone who supports the Body of Christ with their faith; one who drives ministry in a spirit of simplistic trust in God and His power over this world.

If we are unable to do those things fully, then we will receive only a portion, and if we find ourselves reject the teachings of Christ completely, then we have nothing from Him but the dust off his sandals.

We can be there together, however, and have a love for someone else that truly feels unloved. We can have strength for someone who has none, have encouragement for those who are discouraged, and most of all have faith enough for those brothers and sisters who can't seem to find it.

Action Verbs

John 10:1-18 (NIV)
"I tell you the truth, the man who does not enter the sheep pen by the gate, but climbs in by some other way, is a thief and a robber. The man who enters by the gate is the shepherd of his sheep. The watchman opens the gate for him, and the sheep listen to his voice. He calls his own sheep by name and leads them out. When he has brought out all his own, he goes on ahead of them, and his sheep follow him because they know his voice. But they will never follow a stranger; in fact, they will run away from him because they do not recognize a stranger's voice." Jesus used this figure of speech, but they did not understand what he was telling them.

Therefore Jesus said again, "I tell you the truth, I am the gate for the sheep. All who ever came before me were thieves and robbers, but the sheep did not listen to them. I am the gate; whoever enters through me will be saved. He will come in and go out and find pasture. The thief comes only to steal and kill
and destroy; I have come that they may have life and have it to the full.

"I am the good shepherd. The good shepherd lays down his life for the sheep. The hired hand is not the shepherd who owns the sheep. So when he sees the wolf coming, he abandons the sheep and runs away. Then the wolf attacks the flock and scatters it. The man runs away because he is a hired hand and cares nothing for the sheep.

"I am the good shepherd; I know my sheep and my sheep know me just as the Father knows me and I know the Father and I lay down my life for the sheep. I have other sheep that are not of this sheep pen. I must bring them also.

They too will listen to my voice, and there shall be one flock and one shepherd. The reason my Father loves me is that I lay down my life only to take it up again. No one takes it from me, but I lay it down of my own accord. I have authority to lay it down and authority to take it up again. This command I received from my Father."

1 John 3:11-18 (CEV)

From the beginning, you were told that we must love each other. Don't be like Cain, who belonged to the devil and murdered his own brother. Why did he murder him? He did it because his brother was good, and he was evil. My friends, don't be surprised if the people of this world hate you. Our love for each other proves that we have gone from death to life. But if you don't love each other, you are still under the power of death.

If you hate each other, you are murderers, and we know that murderers do not have eternal life. We know what love is because Jesus gave his life for us. That's why we must give our lives for each other. If we have all we need and see one of our own people in need, we must have pity on that person, or else we cannot say we love God. Children, you show love for others by truly helping them, and not merely by talking about it.

From the gospel of John we hear of a wonderful vision that Christ shares with us, and from First John we learn how our actions can shape that to reality. There are so many images we have of Jesus as the good shepherd. My uncle's church was actually called the Episcopal Church of the Good shepherd-- growing up that was one of my earliest understandings of who Christ was. We think of the loving God tending the wayward flock, guiding with the staff, leading to good and wonderful fields of plenty, to streams of good water, protecting us from the robbers and the wolves. The idea of Christ searching us out, no matter the cost, when we are lost and bringing us back into the fold is implanted in our minds.

So often, though, our iconic images can be dead wrong. For instance, this past week I browsed a book a friend loaned me called, "Lies My Teachers Told Me." It re-evaluates the history lessons that we all learned in school and relates the provable fact. One such truth was that the Native Americans of this nation were revered for a time--not consistently fought against. In some of the first few battles, the Native Americans in Ohio would take in the children and women of the frontier men that they had fought against. In the native towns the captured colonists were treated so well that Col. Henry Bouquet writes that when he sought their return, the children to the colonies had to be bound and forcibly returned to white society. The Boston tea party revelers dressed as natives to pay homage to them as to represent themselves as icons of liberty and freedom. In fact the United States seal, which among other symbols, has the eagle holding a clutch of 13 arrows. A symbol that was lifted from the Iroquois League. John Hancock quotes Iroquois advice from 1744. Congress at the time wrote, "The [Iroquois League] are a wise people. Let us hearken to their council and teach our children to follow it."

On that same idea, let us set aside the iconic images about Christ as the shepherd, not so that I can completely disassemble them, but only so that we can get a better look at the meaning of Jesus' parable. The first thing we need to see is Jesus· emphasis in the very first line. I read it to be that Jesus is the Good Shepherd--as opposed to, well, the hired hand which he mentions later. To know a 'good' shepherd we must first understand what it was to be a shepherd. It was not a glorious job. Aside from being one of the most common jobs in ancient times, it was dirty and required much out of the shepherd. It is the shepherd whose hands are bloody with birthing lambs in the spring, and who goes days and weeks without the comforts of home to ensure the sheep have enough to eat and sweet water to drink.

When the sheep are in the sheep pen, it is the shepherd who lies across the door to the pen during the night.

As Jesus says he is willing to do, shepherds were often required to give their lives for the flock. There is a book relating some of the practices of the ancient world written by Dr. WM Thompson. It tells a story about a native Arab shepherd who was taking a flock to Tiberius. He was set upon by nomadic robbers and fought three of them instead of running away. Overpowered, he was actually hacked to pieces by their knives.

The true shepherds never hesitate to lay down their lives for the sheep. Jesus· words here are powerful and emotional. I want you to understand the images that it evoked in the people of the first century and the meaning that it immediately held for them when Christ compares himself to a shepherd. His message here is one of comparisons. The good shepherd lays down his life, while the hired hand abandons the sheep. The hired hand is the one who works only for reward. He thinks chiefly of the money. There is no gain in trying to protect the sheep should he lose and die! Where is his gain? So he runs, leaving the sheepfold. The Good Shepherd though, works not for reward, but for love. And thinks chiefly of the master he is trying to serve. What will we focus on when we are called to serve the master and watch the flock? Our brothers and sisters, our sons and daughters in Christ? Will we seek reward? Will we serve only with the things of the earth on our minds and hearts, or will we forsake these base desires with God-given strength and serve, instead, thinking only of Love. Our scripture from First John, chapter three states, that since Christ was willing to give his life, so too should we be willing to lay down ours for our brothers and sisters. To be as the Good Shepherd was. But how to do this? Not with words, not with feelings of comfort, but with actions. We are told in this passage not to love with the tongue or with words but with actions that come from truth; actions that are truly in the spirit they are intended; actions backed by sincerity. One of the most horrible things we can do to each other is to serve with anger or hate or malice of any type on our hearts. If we serve one another let it be only in real truth.

We have surely failed if we have promised to do one thing, one favor, only to be in the act of doing it with anger or bitterness on our hearts. A pastor once quoted to me that" Bitterness is the vile liquid of the heart that can harden the soul of any saint. "As believers, this passage of John commands us to act only in truth, and in sincerity. How we often break the heart of God when we approach loving acts with steely hearts. To whom then are we to show this kindness, this love, this truthful nature? Christ answered this for us. To whom did He show this kindness and love? He came and died for us, for our sins, but who were we when that happened? We can look to Romans for that. In Romans, Paul describes for us the state we were in when Christ committed the most precious act of love that changed forever the way we must approach one another. In chapter 5 of Romans, we are described as being, without strength. We were totally unable to help ourselves. We were ungodly; we were certainly sinners and still are. Moreover though, Paul describes us as enemies of God. We were rebelling, cursing, neglecting, ignoring, denying and rejecting God. Check out Romans 5:10.

And yet, in this precious story, Christ served as our sacrifice. He took our sin and guilt upon Himself. That was His love. And we are called and commanded to act in love following His example. We must love people just as he did. We must love them even when they oppose us and do things against us and are our enemies--just as we were once enemies to God! Now that means that we do not only tolerate them, but that also does not mean that we pray only for them, it means we love them, like our own kin, like our own children like our own mothers and fathers. Love, in action, and love that comes from truthful sincerity.

One of the first missionaries to the Native Americans was Egerton Young in Saskatchewan. To the Native Americans, the story of God's love was an amazing one and a new revelation. After Young had told his story, the chief asked him, 'Just now you told us about the Great Spirit who created all things, did I hear you say Our Father? Young replied that he had said that. The chief replied, 'That is new and very sweet to me. We never thought of the Great Spirit as father, we saw Him in the lightning and the power of His world and sometimes feared him, but never before saw that He was a loving Father. Did you say just now that He is also your father?

Again Young said yes, that was true. The chief asked further, "And you also said that he was my native people's father?" Again yes. Then a smile broke on the chief's face, and in a bark of joy he shouted, "Then you and I are brothers!"

We are truly the family of God. Brothers and sisters to one another. Not just to the ones in our individual church congregations, but every person in your city, in your state, and on and on.

Christ shared with us this vision, this dream that he prophesied from God, this story that he tells with love: all the sheep in one sheepfold with Him guarding at the gate. We are called to lives of action. Of prayer and worship certainly, but foremost, we must have lives of action to go out and love those who oppose us--not with tracts or words, or even prayers, though all those things have their place. We must act, and those actions must reflect the truth that is in our hearts.

The importance of this is that if we do not, if we cannot bring ourselves to love those who oppose us then we do not know the love of Christ. We must work against the visceral human feeling we have to people that oppose us and instead temper that with the divine love.

Our faith does not reside in our churches. Those are where we worship, our communal gathering place for strength and fellowship. Our faith is outside those buildings--in every action, in every other brother and sister outside those walls, those who oppose us, who dares us to love them. We must answer the call; to reply to that defiance with the love and truth that we learn from Christ, or truly, we cannot claim to know Jesus.

Because that was His mission. To keep the flock from being scattered, to lie against the gate of the sheepfold in protection, to seek out the lost sheep and to bring the other sheep that are not of this pen! For there is one flock and one shepherd. But it begins with us. It is with us that Christ shared this vision, and it is our actions and the sincerity of our hearts that has the power to realize that vision and bring it to pass in this lifetime--not with concern or words, but with action forged in truth and tempered in the fire of the love of our God.

Poems

Oceana

There were waves of softest blue.
Welling deep within them
was the darkness of every night,
as they rolled into the shores.

There was the crunch in the grains of sand,
pooled magic left in the in-step's impression.

Walking toward thunder.
Hurling.
Fleeing.

Into the push of the waves and the
pull of the brine's arms.

The wanting of the Sea.

The foam around her eyes,
weeping bitter tears for every dream ever lost,
and everyone never found,
and everyone never started.

There were couples who stood on her shores.
Separated by her depth,
broken by her vastness,
embittered by her time.
How many couples promised?

With their feet rooted in Her water,
connected by her wind,
stroked by her knell,
made whole by her kiss.

Snowfall

I contemplate the paths of a stonework in winter.
I saw two staircases that led to the same door.
My path splits before me to follow the two
Joining again at the top of the door.
The footprints before me evenly tread
To my left and right, merging ahead.
I stand and I think of the spring, of the thaw,
When all of these same footprints have gone on before.
But I picked a path without one other thought
Of who'd preceded my path and reach the door that I sought.
But now I stand worried, I'm wondering why,
What things made these footprints?
Pick the paths that I saw.
Was it quickness, or safety, or deed without thought?
And the questions continue as I stand out and freeze
unable to move or to choose my own path.
For I realize that always, when I step in the snow,
If I walk on the path to where I may go
I never will lead, but only follow.
But even in spring, I think of it now,
I've always been following those footprints I see
Though I've never once thought it, as I hurry along.
So I continue to stand and between the two stairs
As to which one I will choose;
I walk straight and sure up over the rail,
For in leading there's nothing to lose.

Is it Fall?

Flying between the rust in trees
The sun catches the tips of uncountable leaves,
those flecks of color
Sticks support them, shooting into the dark
where the sun won't reach
Branches like frozen auburn lightning in the light
like broken gray arms out of shadow
the bone of a bare white sycamore shouting out against them
Sailing through the high in hills
The light of a sun that sets, capping the rolls of earth
Golds of the ground peeking out to the darkening highlands
Clothing them with the yellow orange of a master's touch.
Floating over the valley that houses jutting myriads of color
Dusty colored grasses backing a collage of autumn flavors
Reds, browns, golds, orange and lingering green.

Unkind Air

I can feel the wind again,
blowing as before.
Mocking me from the unseen world,
knowing.
Its breath is like laughter,
smiling at me in my fix.
I wonder what to do as it
brings back that night I thought I'd left
a night that withheld it's causes
until the ray of morning shown
(or, in less romantic fields,
the vacuum swept outside)
I lifted my hindrance, of the feeling I had
for one night and let you see
what I'd want in that perfect world
or was it what would never be?
I feel it, even now, as I touch your face
or course my hand through your hair.
And wonder what will come--will come?
What of my lady fair?
Still, I breathe your scent and breathe,
still, I feel your hand«
As I see every glimmer of what you are
I feel that much further from you.
What of you, dear? I'd ask you,
if in that perfect world we trod.

Though here, I sit and wonder what
you feel 'neath your facade.
Perhaps it's not my place to say,
or p 'raps it's only I, who can,
that with him your face is set in stone. . .
Is it hiding what's below?
I ask only for your sake, not for mine,
as only I contend,

That yours should be undaunted bliss--
Not something in constant mend.
What do you mean? The wind breaths back
mocking me in truth,
For I only say what these eyes bring,
and what they hold isn't eternally sincere.
Still the wind blows, cold and hard,
as it did outside that night.
Biting me, did you forget?
Or was I, never right?

As I sit behind you

I find myself in gaze at the
sight of your figure near me
a curl of hair, to my eye,
is all but a twist of comfort
against a public will I feel
my had in yours;
the soft of your hands holding mine.
Like some lover who rests across the expanse of the ocean
I see your likeness in my thoughts.
As if some long warring soldier
I yearn for the moment I'd hold you.
Like a man, unjustly chained, in a foreign prison
Your feet dance with mine on the sand of imagined beaches
The footprints left behind are a sad memory of the dancers
and the love that the song shared with them.

Ode to dead petals on my floor; dedicated to no-one

how am i supposed to write
with this bussing in my ear?
how can i compose
an "ode to the tulip" if you won't stop
TALKNING TO ME
I appreciate that you think
you need
to have my opinion, BUT
I'd really rather not,
I want to make a story
about what happened
to me to-day, BUT
you are telling me about the past
and i can't look ahead
so I'm sitting here in dread
of what you'll say next.
I was just in someone's room where it was quiet and nice
and then i come back here to write what i was thinking
and YOU are in my way
YOU'RE obstructing my masterpiece.
I'm suing you for one billion-million dollars
cause that is how much i would have made
if YOU weren't in my way
so now the tulip died and I'm tired and
all i wanted was for YOU to be quiet.
so I'll write an "ode to dead petals on my floor" instead
and i won't even dedicate it to you.

You can't trust flowers
"She loves me, she loves me not."
A yellow daisy never lies.
So, I must know what she thinks
And pluck these petals from this eye.
She watches just the flower,
This tiny yellow bud of spring,
And biting her lip she waits and wonders
What message it will bring
Then, with half its petals gone,
It is crushed within her own hand,
She keeps it on mine, the flower between,
And brings her eyes from it to me.
She purses her lips and brings them,
Oh so sweet, to mine; such bliss!
And after that cosmic brilliance says,
"Don't trust a flower with this."

Will these fingers type ever faster?

To keep the rhythm of a pounding soul in line
As if pulsing to some unseen drum of time,
the mind works harder and faster
Against the unseen foe.
It waters away at the defenses
Make the heart unloved and slow
And naught will save you from this gloomy death,
No potion salve or herb
Naught but your prayer to God above
Could save you from the dying love.
Like a plague in corporeal form it beats at the breast of the war
torn
It knows what it will find there--horrors unseen by other men
The plague knows who it's the rests are
(oh! Gifted fingers write ever faster! 'Fore this dreaded Life
Consume thee and twists thine bones into Its way.
Speak on dear fingers of Truth, Speak on! For you alone
Are left, you alone have the words to bring
The Love of life back to the War-Torn....)
The drums disguise the plague as it comes,
Knocking upon the breast
Of each human in its way.
It wants those who would usurp its power
By truly living in this life.
By loving all who seek and come
This is what will leave the page undone.
And so it fights, on and on against the tired
And weary battlers, who had stood a thousand years and,
by their God, will stand a thousand more.

Out Dancing

You see her,
the smug little queen
Standing on the stair,
Moving to the music
Disregarding the advances
of the riffraff with a glance.
still pictures of her
are etched in your mind

-for a moment-
in sync with the strobe light and bass.

You can see her in the mirror,
like an MTV re-run spirit
then with your ears throbbing
harder than the level
you look around
at all these other people --
You are not in your element
your tribal dance and dress
always seem out of place
here in the city
it is only sorely evident now.
The beat seems similar first,
but then the rhythm is corrupted
you can't move like they do anymore,
the syncopated gyrating.
A part of you says to stop saving yourself
-- to drink,
and dance
and screw
and may your life be short.
But the poet in you won't let that happen.
You are to see,
Record,

meditate
up until the end of your minutes.
And when the dancing
is done
and morning has come
and the beat --
a monstrous beast of swirling color --
It's coming inland from the far sea.
It seems odd at first,
then alluring,
then passionate,
then consuming.
then off-harmony,
then distasteful,
then poisonous,
then finally like the beating
of the tell-tale heart.
Throbbing you into insanity
your soul starts itching for air
before being overwhelmed
by the city's essence.
Filling your lungs
sucking you dry,
empty,
yearning fullness.

Shadeless Room

Shadows dancing on the wall
Flicker in and out
Can't hear a word of what you're saying
I'm the stranger in your foreign place.
Just feel the rhythm
The rhyme,
The time.
Can't hear about the passionate woes,
The love that was lost,
The nights up drinking.
Through the smoky haze, the world seems the same.
But all I really have
Are shadows dancing on the walls.

Smoke

Has the smoke become so thick?
Or the music far too loud?
Come home, your roots call you,
Born of the past
For you won't ever smile again
Hanging on to what's not you or yours.
Let the old songs fill you
Lift you in harmony
Listen to how your music made love
The fair girl that past 2 the youth that smiled back
How the wine closed your eyes
And you dreamed of future times
Remember all the times you fought
To hang on to what was yours
The women that raised sons to fight for you
Against those who would possess you.
The men who marched, the boys,
Who let blood and glory fall?
For the chance to be with you.

Reflections

Clutching instead of holding
Living instead of fleeing
Forgiving and falling
And running and breathing
And going places and going
No-where
To the Lighthouse,
To the boathouse,
To the beach-house my friend.
To every place I'd ever dreamed, we'd go.
I wanted to leave my shoes by the doorway
Leave a trail of clothes we'd thrown
And wake up to good mornings
Every spring from now till ever
I'll fall in love with you
All over again.
With fresh winds and newness
All around
The same new feeling
Again
With all the lilac breaths I breathe
Every Flower pressed,
Lupine, Old Wolf, New growth, fingers, rings,
Streams, dogwoods, books, hats, smiles, snowflakes,
Snow Angels, Rain Angels, winds, suns, moons, stars,
Rainbows, paints, eyes, pictures, hanging upside down,
Writing upside down, laying and talking upside down,
Marshmallows and pretzels and praying
And old moments, and new ones.

Moule Cafe

In a twilight coffee house
Under light. Soft amber glow.
Eyes look out quietly.
Under hair. Brown
Bringing soft beauty
To a Colder type of day.
Sits. Dark green shirt.
Brushing crumbs. Stretching out
After chewing with her mouth open.
Flipping hair, collecting plates.
Walking to the back room.
Donning apron. Coming out.
  "Can I get you anything?"

psalm 101

Lord of Wind and Air,
Breath and Spirit.
You who may set fire to the clouds
Who shone within the sun as
Life-bringer, Light-giver.
My love for you is more than my
human frame 2 with all its weakness 2
can dare to endure.
With my spirit open I can speak
without fear of my love for you.
In You I am truly blest,
without, I am in black despair.
How great are the Blessings of Your Soul,
Dear Lord. Above and all around me
You exist as the Wind and Everything
my eyes could behold.
May my simple mouth
forever lift You up in Praise.

RSS Fed

I don't feel like writing a poem.
I don't feel like writing anything
I feel like sleeping.
Sleeping so hard that I would die
For just a little while
And wake up to a new day
Another lifetime that I would be leading.
Same places
Same soul
Different only on the outside of the outside
Different only in places that I would never realize
I feel like being mindless.
Like letting my brain swim around for while
Processing
Trying to believe
Trying to make magic work again in this world
Trying to deny science and reason
My soul sleeps, waiting.

A truth of zeros

even
incorporate.
inconceivably,
inconsequentially,
Indecisively,
Even.
Scores are set to 0
chalked on slates
wiped clean.
The weather's mild
not adult or child
Colors gray.
And all you
are
is
Even.

Sock drawers

Memories
flitting daily to torture
mindfulness that have been brought along
like luggage.
Things saying and asking« Come back!
Where have you been?
Old feelings like socks stuffed under the bed and rediscovered.
lowercase letters filling too much room, in a place the begs
understanding.
odd things.
Only reality stands strong and says,
it never was this way.
Socks have a way of changing with time into
not what was,
but to what might have been
Hindsight being what it is« perfect.
Things are always so much nicer.
Like picture albums of life, only ever recording the fun and
fantastic memories that were had.
Our Albums should be more truthful.
When we fight, grab the camera.
When we bicker, pop the flash.
How much would we rant when we knew
that we would look back at it in years to come
and remember the time when there was truth

So scared

Someday
because of our obsession
with the Bogeyman
Everyone will stop seeing the stars
The starry nights will be
forgotten.
made
into stories
like Noah and his flood.
truthfully, we fear
the Bogeyman still.
We never will out-grow him
So we put streetlights
and stop lights
and house lights
and flashlights
and store lights
and security lights
and bar lights
and lamp light.
Until there's not a
Shred of Shadow
MR. Boogey could use.
But in
protecting
ourselves
from the
nightmare--
we destroy any chance
at the
dream
So when we stand
in the streets
protected by
our lights

we look up
and see
nothing
and remember the funny
amusing stories
about the
stars.

Short Fiction

Shift

Awakenings:

"Jeff? Jeff, wake up. It's your turn to drive."

Somewhere from the foggy recluse of uncomfortable sleep in a car, Jeff heard the small voice before he felt the hand on him. There was a breeze coming in through the open door as he raised his head and blinked his eyes blearily. With her sing-songy voice, Kala had awakened him and already held the keys out in front of him, her eyebrows raised, jingling them impatiently.

"Okay, okay." Jeff groaned, getting out of his seat and taking the keys, "Where are we?" He stood up and looked at the McDonald's they were parked beside as he stretched his back.

"Outside of Canton, a few miles before Newcomerstown and the highway exit. Think you can handle the drive?" Kala said jokingly as she walked around to the already open trunk smiling.

"I hope so." Jeff said under his breath as he stretched again. It was a roadside Mickey-D's with a little turquoise flair and not much else. The lot was deserted except for one of those cliché red convertibles parked diagonally from them on the street side of the lot.

"I'm going in to wash up. Be right back." He started off, then, as an after-thought, he called back still walking forward, "Do you want anything?" He saw her close the trunk and shake her head "no" before he got to the door.

Movie Rights:

They were large breasts. Pushed up into a white tee shirt with neatly store-hemmed sleeves that denoted more class than just a cotton jersey. They were the kind of breasts that made Jeff stop in his mind as he reached for the door and internally cry out Oh my-- but he couldn't finish because he realizes that the thought is too vulgar to be associated with his idea of God. She came out of the car -- the only other one on the lot -- and strode towards him and the door. His eyes followed her in a "too good to be real" awe as she closed the distance between him and the eatery. The tee was tucked neatly into a pair of stone wash blues, which melted over wide hips. There was curly blond hair that complemented a toothy smile. Jeff held the door far too long for her, just to catch another glimpse in the hope that she wouldn't notice him taking her in. She was so far from the door when he started holding it, so that she felt obligated to jog the last few feet towards him. She whispered a note of thanks as Jeff tried to tell himself that held the door for purely gentlemanly purposes.

In All the Wrong Places:

In the bathroom Jeff stared blankly at the tile wall, his mind going on about the girl that had gone into the bathroom across from him. He stood there with his thing in his hands thinking about how she was just in the next room and how he could, or should, say something to her on the way out. As he washed, he tried to convince himself in the mirror that he wouldn't ever see her again, no one in the area knew him, for him to be humiliated in front of. Just say something, he kept telling himself. Anything. Excuse me ma'am, I just had to tell you that I'm not some perverted psycho out on the road, but you are one of the most beautiful women I have ever encountered. That was true. It wasn't just the way she looked; there was something -- wild, alluring, about the way she walked and smiled at him unafraid. Walking out of the bathroom he met her there, just before going into the main restaurant. He held the door for her again, said absolutely nothing as she thanked him, bought something to eat and left.

Newcomerstown:

Driving through the little town gave Kala enough reason to stay awake, at least for a little while. She chattered on, or did what seemed to Jeff to be chatter, about her family and how many times they had driven through this same town, the places that they had stopped, the different things that they had seen each time. Jeff silently munched on his fries and nodded when it was appropriate. She went on, and on until Jeff's prayer was answered -- they came onto the highway and she began to drift off to sleep.

Mile 632:

Jeff glanced at the marker on the side of the road while he tried to merge with the oncoming traffic. Merging had become some kind of bizarre ballet in Jeff's mind through his years of driving. Blinker on, three glances, ahead, behind, the mirror, behind again, hit the gas, too much, pump the brake; the motions of the transition had all of the awkwardness of the first-time passions, with none of the beauty or romance. Here on the road, each person, each family, each couple was reduced to their own environment within the vehicle, and a boxy representation to the world on the outside. You weren't people. You were vehicles. While driving Jeff cursed and swore at the tiniest infraction to what he considered to be his religious right to his share of the road. But he wasn't screaming at people, he was screaming at cars. The one that cuts him off isn't a grandmother who's in a hurry to see the newest grandchild, she's demon in an Oldsmobile. Jeff kicked off the sandals he was wearing, letting the cruise take control of the car for a moment, and put his bare toes back on the pedal feeling the ridges of the rubber with his feet. He shut off the cruise. He hated letting the car drive for him; he liked the weight of the pedal pushing back against his feet. It felt mindless to do it any other way.

It wasn't cold outside, just chilly really. Kala was wrapped up in a blanket as she sat in the bucket seat beside him and warm air oozed out of the floor vent and partly up Jeff's pant leg. The heat had to ooze out of this jalopy, the fan was broken, though the heater worked, so the faster you drove the more air came out of the registers. Jeff usually had it up to 74, regardless of the limit. He was the kind of person that wholly believed that as long as he kept an eye out, he would see the police before they saw him. So far, he had been right. He had never gotten a ticket but was smart enough to know that someday his number would be up; the thrill of driving outweighed the danger of being caught.

Jeff liked driving. He liked marking cars as he passed them, he liked being nose to nose before he pushed his Chevy to the limit to pass them. He liked driving in the dark pre-dawn hours where curves, that you were going too fast for, would sneak up on you, pushing their g-force against you as you fought for control. He was actually conceited--one of those drivers that you might start to pass but as soon as they realize what you're doing they quit their daydreaming and resume an un-passable speed. Jeff also liked seeing cars that he had passed playing along with him. He would see them again in his rear-view mirror and think about how they were going to try again to pass him. He would let them get close on purpose, when he was really playing, and then take off just as they began to eek past him.

Mile 598:

It had been over 30 minutes since Jeff first came onto the road; his mind had started wandering. He wanted to know why he had not said anything to a beautiful young woman an hour before. He wanted to know what inhibiting factors kept his mouth shut and his head down while he saw her closely. He remembered her face vaguely, as if his mind was already reconstructing it into something more familiar. He realized that his mind often reconstructed its own memories into things that were more familiar if he didn't have enough time to let himself truly register something. A song that he would hear for the first time in passing would change itself into a more familiar tune, a name would find itself not as it was, and instead the name of a cousin or an uncle was used in its place. In the case of the Fast Food Girl, the name his mind had come up with, Jeff felt that this replacement was a real tragedy. All he was left with were the emotions he held of their pseudo-meeting.

Mile 530:

At some point during a drive the scenery gets boring. It doesn't depend on where you are or where you are going, it is simply a fact that much of an area within a 300-mile radius very closely resembles itself along the highway. In the blur of speed, everything gets mushed together and it is impossible to distinguish the traits of trees and rocks and critters that you know are there. Your mind starts searching for a subject, so Jeff began to daydream. Fast Food Girl. She hadn't had a special someone waiting for her inside the eatery, that much was real truth. Though, from McDonald's she had somehow gotten ahead of him, perhaps not taking so much time in Newcomerstown, and then there she was up ahead, stopped on the side of the road. Jeff looked to the seat beside him -- maybe Kala wasn't here. So, being the chivalrous person that he was, Jeff pulled over in front of her stopped '89 Ford mustang; it was odd that in all of his daydreams the cars were usually Fords. She smiled as she saw who it was stopping for her and waved in an embarrassed way.

What about her voice, how would she sound? It was sweet, but husky, it said "hi" in such a way that the word got lost over the curve of her lips, as if even the word didn't want to leave her sweetened tongue. She had her hands in her pockets with her thumbs sticking out, looking off to the side in that kind of Well-this-is-really-embarrassing-but, look.

"Having trouble?" Jeff said in an all too cliché and "B" movie way. "Yeah," and then she stated the kind of trouble she was having and in this particular daydream Jeff knew all about cars and could help her out of this situation, as opposed to the reality in which he would simply give her a lift. Suddenly this was the more attractive of the two ideas.

So, she got into the car, completely trusting in her "wild-child" way, as Jeff drove her to the next town. Her hair smelled like -- he paused. He was stumped. He tried to think of the best smell on a woman he had ever breathed. Then he remembered.

Mile 476:

The lakeside. Water was warm and the bugs weren't out this time of year. She was standing there beside him looking out over the water that they were in up to their knees. He smiled as he thought of the wind in her hair, her hair in his face. He remembered the smell of it as he held her. It was bittersweet like tasting a good chili, all ancho chilies and brown sugar over tart tomatoes. It was filling, it had a flavor all its own, it wanted you to breath in more of it as you inhaled.

"These have been some of the happiest times of my life." He remembered thinking it, not saying it, but hoped that she had heard just as if his mouth had moved. There was a wind that night that made small waves in the lake's calm waters, and it was a large enough lake that the sun had room to close the water around itself as it sank. They stood, walked, took stones from the shore and enjoyed the company of one another. It was as close to bliss as Jeff could imagine or remember himself being. Kala roused. She stretched some as Jeff's mind snapped back to where he was, the lake and the sun and the woman being tucked back into their place.

"Where are we?" She asked in the stretching squeak of someone who had their back arched.

"Just passed the exit for Zelienople." Jeff replied, amused at her Sound.

"Mmmm." She leaned over and put her head on Jeff's lap, the blanket still around her shoulders.

Mile 303:

Jeff hummed and tapped his fingers on the steering wheel. He looked down at Kara lying in his lap, the music in his head fading off as he started thinking again. Kara always slept in the car, so there was never music playing while they drove together. Jeff scowled unconsciously at the sleeping woman. He wondered, as she slept, why he wasn't content with her. He really knew somewhere in some part of his soul that it just wasn't appropriate to look at while driving.

There are rules to how deep you can forage within yourself while you're on the road. Somewhere, Jeff believed, the National Highway Bureau had the specs on it. He looked from the road back to her. Kara didn't move him. She was the kind of woman that had excellent credentials: considerate, pretty, sweet, not a goody-two-shoes, but kind enough, thoughtful of him. She simply didn't make stars turn, the earth moves, the rainbows shine. She didn't have it within her to make story book romances tarnish in envy of the love she inspired. Jeff snorted at himself and shook his head. Wasn't that how it was supposed to work? Jeff, he knew he was expecting too much out of her, out of all women. Secretly he hoped he was wrong, but he suspected he wasn't.

All he really wanted, he realized was someone who actually heard him. Someone who was mindful of his emotions, not just interested in them. Someone that didn't fit credentials but fit him. He was always looking for that special someone and would often get impatient with a relationship if it wasn't moving him in the way he thought it should. He didn't really like being on this quest; a glorious cause he felt driven into. He was getting tired of seeking or searching.

Which is why he was here, in this car, driving a sleeping girl around Ohio, wishing that she would talk to him, that he could listen to music and drown out his thoughts, that the trip would be over and he could stop thinking, that he would stop fantasizing about women he brushed in life because what he came up with in his head was infinitely more interesting than what was happening to two people in a car in Ohio, amidst hundreds of others on the road probably wishing the same thing.

Mile 278:

Jeff's heart was drumming in his ears as his armpits suddenly dripped sweat into his shirt.

"I'm sorry." He stared straight at the road, not wanting to look at Kara again as she fumed out of the window. She shook her head. "It's a wide road, Jeff." Her head twitched with birdlike angularity.

"I. Am. Sorry." Jeff's words were slow, deliberate and for the fifth time. He had made up a story about someone cutting him off, since the truth that he was fantasizing about imaginary women was inconceivable to relate.

"Fine." She was inches from the stick shift, and worlds away from her boyfriend.

Jeff began thinking about a war. A battle between mind and soul, heaven and hell. This line of thinking was strictly forbidden as too deep for the Auto-Philosopher -- you ran the danger of putting yourself to sleep or driving yourself into a guardrail.

Though Jeff's mind was fixed on the brutality of such a war. He was sure that at some point in history there must have been a real war that was half as fervent as he was imagining his to be. To have two sides so eternally pitted against each other, to have each side knowing with all of their heart and soul that it was they who were the side of right. He thought of Holy wars, the Jihads in which men would gladly blow themselves to smithereens in the name of their Sovereign God.

In his head there were two such sides, already rushing, screaming and furious, into a battle. The lords of the war hung back to give orders and snap commands. Bloodied faces crashed into each other as a screaming sea of flesh and weapons came together in a horrific theater of gore. This was the ignoble part of war. The part that isn't painted in history books. In school Jeff had been shown all of the treaties being signed, the swords handed over -- he remembered that. But he knew there was more. He knew that men possessed a hatred, a part of themselves kept under lock and key. The part that created those fabulous machines. Hurling metal and wood at the object of hatred. History never showed what was happening here, on the road inside his head. A private war of screams and light and flashes of powder that is blotted out as another body falls over your face. The crushing weight of it all robs you of the ability to find the breath to cry out that you are still alive as more limbs are piled atop you.

The road on which Jeff drove, was a battlefield full of machines. Each car doing what hatred does for the foot soldiers. They made people stop being real. On the other side there are no brothers or fathers, or me who laughed with children. There were only enemies. There were only sterile cars coming at you, devoid of life, secreting away the humanity locked inside of it. And there, on the field, there is one soldier who clears a way through flesh like a gardener reaping through so many contorting fleshy vines; this one man has become the epitome of a reaper. Consuming the nameless faces before him. advancing. Making better machines, training faster men, building force, growing to immense proportion feeding on the nourishment of inane hatred. The forces opposing him fall in sheaves of terrible panicked fear. His animal, his secret inside, has become alight with the will to do more than survive. He is fire, uncontrolled, only wanting to live; consuming anything that even whispers a threat to that life. Consuming with the insatiable hunger of oceans. There is a sea-like foam on his bloodied lips that sprays a breaker as he roars from a deep anguish that he does not yet understand. A death cry to every obstacle of muscle and bone before him. Then this man, this epitome of rage, stopped. Atop a mountain

of flesh and hatred in Jeff's mind, the warrior surveyed what laid around him, and the fury in the sky rolled away. Animal eyes left him. And as humanity breathed through the body again the man saw. He crumpled as if the anger had been the blood in his veins. His massive frame withered as he had look around him and seen faces. Here the hand of a man who fixed a boat to sail again on sunny Mediterranean waters. There the chest of a man who breathed deeply in mountains few ever saw. There the legs of man who had been busy at his business. There a face, a pair of eyes, part of a life, part of a person. All lying around him. Nothing was worth the price paid on the battlefield. Nothing was worth the fact that bits and pieces of life had been slain in the name of survival. Every warrior was unworthy, humbled, anguished. this one was no different. He became a warning, a walking nightmare of own self-inflicted horror haunted by the war he had waged.

And, of course, Jeff knew that if he ever dared allow his mind to assign a face to that man, it was his own face. And the face of nearly everyone he knew.

Refueled:

"Do you want anything?" Kala spoke over the hood of the car before she went in.

"I'm fine, go ahead and pay the $12.00 too." Jeff was doing his duty as a male and "manning" the pump.

"Are you going to get it even?" Jeff stared at her blankly. He prided himself on the fact that his pumping skill always had the number add up to an even dollar. Kara rolled her eyes.

"Okay, sorry. Be right back." He watched her go and started to outline what he would think about once they were underway again. How he wanted to analyze his relationship with her, where it was going, where it had been, why he had asked her out in the first place. Things that he could only do while she slept, while she was there, beside him, on his mind.

"You don't mind if I go back to sleep, do you?" Kala asked as she was already settling in, pulling up the blanket over her shoulders, making it clear that nearly nothing he could say was going to stop her. Jeff simply replied the dutiful and expected, "No, I'm fine."

"You could turn on the radio, you know. It won't bother me."

"No, I'm okay, really" She turned to him and looked curiously, "How do you just sit

there and drive with nothing to listen to?"

He smiled, "I just think," he replied.

"Sometimes I think you think too much." Kala turned back over and settle in as Jeff started the car and sped up the on ramp.

MaryAnn

She walked. Long librarian legs stuffed up under a shortish brown skirt. To talk to her I never would have thought her the sort that would wear stocking hose. But she was. The lady that I knew she was, chit chatted over the stacks of checkouts I had made just to have her spend those few moments smiling at me. Ask her name . . .

"There you go." She slides my stack forward.

"Thanks," I gather them up, "Say, uh... I didn't really catch your name." I want to crawl in a hole. I wished it were true that nobody really says those things anymore. She smiles. Plays along. That smile.

"I don't remember throwing it." She laughs. Caught off guard, I twitter back.

Idiot! What is the magical pheromone that reduces grown men to addled preschoolers? I might as well have said "boogers" and kicked her in the shin.

"I'll tell you but only if you promise me not to laugh."

She waits. I agree. "MaryAnn."

I smile. "MaryAnn the Librarian."

"You promised not to laugh." She frowned but smiling.

Complicated. But she does it. Somehow.

"Ok. I wasn't laughing. Just . . . Amused. Sorry. You're sure you aren't putting me on?"

"Do you want to see my ID?" She tilted her head and smiled a little deeper. Challenging.

"Ah, heh, no no. You seem trustworthy." There is a pause in which I notice her: long hands, bright eyes, slender neck . . . all beautiful and becoming. Lady like. "Well," I break the quiet with expected cordiality, "thanks for these." I smile. I pick up the books, leave my card on purpose, and walk out of the double doors wanting to take one lingering look at MaryAnn the Librarian, but resisting.

Asspettere la Bella

In the distance over speakers that had become tinny with their age, was playing a song from "The Sound of Music." It was one of those melodies that you recognized immediately, but only on some other conscious level. Four young students played Putt Golf beneath the music, obvious to it for the most part and enraptured in a world made up of their own relationships. On the seventh hole of the course Lynn gripped her club, intensely lining up her view towards the hole and beyond the heart shaped turf, taking practice swings. There was a friendly competitive edge to these almost tradition games these four played yearly. Lynn, a medium brunette of almost any description, was currently holding the group longer at a hole that was notorious for foiling her game. The Heart green had especially precarious slopes. The other three generally took a few swings and gave in to the max strokes, ready to move on. Lynn seemed determined this year.

"This isn't the U.S. Open or something, just putt." Daniel's voice was agitated.

Not taking her eyes off the hole Lynn retorted, "First off; the U.S. Open is tennis, not golf, and I can take as much time as I want."

Daniel rolled his eyes, "Fine, we're going to start the next hole." He turned from the course and tugged on his sister's sleeve. "And there are Opens in both; golf and tennis," he shot back over his shoulder.

"Whatever." She bit into her lip and tapped the ball. It rolled up the heart incline and against the wall. "Damnit." She hung her head and throttled the club in near-mock anguish.

David, her senior by many years, and who had stayed behind from Daniel and his sister, couldn't resist. "You know for as long as you line up your shots, I would have thought that you would putt better than that." Lynn narrowed her eyes at David as she followed her ball over the heart but gave in with a smirk.

"For as many wise ass remarks as you make, I'd think you'd be funnier." Lynn's focus went back to the ball. David smiled back as she lined it up. He loved this. The game between friends, being able to spend time on the Ohio lakefront, the mornings of fog; it was the seventh year that be had been able to come. Somehow, he felt that with his graduating college next year this would probably be his last time to stay for a whole week. The possibilities of a permanent job and the start of grad school loomed on the horizon like a dream that wasn't real; a forest

through and evening gloom. Lynn putted again, and again -- despite her best efforts -- the ball went wide. With a small growl she made the traditional last putt: scooping the ball into the hole.

"There. Stupid hole." She readjusted her ball cap.

"So, that would be 6?" David couldn't help himself.

"Yes. Nasty thing." For a moment she faked pouting as she scooped up her ball from the hole. As the started down the little path to Hole 8, she grabbed David's arm quickly. "Thanks for waiting with me."

"Well..." was all David could think to say as he patted her arm.

In truth, having Lynn here made his love for the Lakeside that much stronger. She had always intoxicated him. She was a mystery. As the group started into the next hole, David ignored Danielis annoyed and passing glance, and thought fondly of the first time her really got to know her. The rest of the game passed in a blur. David trying his best to curtail his flirtations with Lynn in order to minimize the hostility he felt from Daniel, and at the same time trying to fulfill the need he had to express and assuage his feelings for her.

Someone suggested ice cream from a locally famous place on their walk back to the cottages. While she decided, ordered, and reached over to grab her cone form the vendor David couldn't help watching her. He wanted to record her every movement, he wanted to dissect the way she made him feel, understand what power she held over him. Often times he admonished himself for being far too romantic of mind and tried desperately to tell himself that he was simply falling into some imagined area of fascination that poets had long warned man about. He would tell himself that it was too story book, that it was too whimsical. Yet, there it was. Exactly as the poets described. It was powerful and pulling. His feelings for her was truly the ocean, it was truly the comfort on nights alone.

It was at these times of self-disclosure he would remind himself of the tragic truth. She knew none of it. At least he assumed. In his fondest hopes he knew that she knew, and of course felt the return, but, as he was, she too was held back by other feelings. Held in place by friends' disapproval and family's questions. Or imagined questions.

Dancing. Dreams of dancing. He was having them again. He could see her standing and smiling. Anticipant and nervous at their crossing the dance floor together for the first time. He reached out. Him first, always him first. But he took her, her hand lightly, so lightly, in his hand. He was thinking in the dream Tighter; I need to feel your hand. Hold on tighter. But the grip never came. They were whirling and whirling along the floor. There were feelings, longing, elations, foreboding. The nervousness, her laughter, mixing and mingling. I'm going to drop her, she's going to fall, don't drop her, not yet. Hold on to me. Hold on...

A tiny boom box in the corner cranked out whatever pop mix was most recently topping the charts as a pair challenged each other in Rummy. The music was lost on these two, their attention on the game at hand.

"What's your middle name?" Lynn was leaning back in the deck chair looking at him when she asked.

"Why?" David stared at his cards.

"Color me curious."

"Is that orange?" Playfully he narrowed his eyes, thinking, "Green maybe? I forget." He ran his tongue over his eyetooth and laid down three kings, and looked back at his

Cards. "Just tell me." She cocked her head in the universal gesture for come on.

"Tats-a-mammal-haught." He kept his head down.

"Are you serious?" her voice said she nearly believed him. He looked up from his cards and grinned.

"It's your turn, and no, I'm not. It's Sean."

"You're a dork." She drew a card from the deck and looked at in her hand.

"You almost believed me."

"Well how was I supposed to know! You have all the Pakistani background or something." She rearranged some things with her cards.

"Iranian." He corrected her, slightly wounded she hadn't remembered. "So, how about you?"

"Lynn." She replied evenly concentrating on the game for a minute.

"Right. Ok, I see. Middle name. I gave you mine."

"It really is Lynn." She laid down a few aces and a wild card; along with a wicked smile "That'd be 45 more points, and your turn."

He stared at his cards for a moment before taking a few cards off the discard pile, "Ok Lynn, so, then," he paused, "what's your first name?" He looked up from his hand. "Or am I allowed to know?"

"Cassius." She replied quickly and smiled. He shook his head. "You know, by following my jokes like this -- I expect better from you."

She simply grinned wickedly. "You discarding or something?" She blinked innocently. He laid down three sixes and put a two in the pile. "And besides," she reached for his two, "it really is Cassius. My dad has a thing for boxing."

"Are you serious? Cassius Clay? He named you after Cassius Clay?" Still looking at her cards Lynn raised her eyebrow with a tight-lipped grin.

David asked again, "You're really not kidding?"

"No. And I'm also out." She laid down three kings and discarded a nine.

David paused, looking at his fairly enormous hand. "And you also suck."

Lynn laughed. He just smiled and stared at her smile -- feeling stupid as he did it, but not stopping in the meantime.

They stood together in the woods for the first time. He was teaching her to run. He loved the idea that she could. The woodland was bathed in light, dusk or dawn. Mysterious golden light that only can come in dreams. They were at the top of a hill in the autumn. The leaves were around them, there was a tiny chorus of the breeze and forest sounds weaving in and out of the trees. Come with me. He says. Follow, follow, run and fly down the hill. Don't look down, leap! Leap! Now RUN. Let the hill catch you, let the mountain hold on to you. Share my magic. Share with me.

Then, just before the dream ends there is one clear thought never before, and probably never again, would he find her.

There was soft jazz playing over the brand-new radio, the smell of car upholstery coming up around bucket seats. The car was in the garage, but Lynn and David were miles away. She was lost somewhere in telling him about this most exciting life event. He was lost in her.

"Fifty-seven miles on it so far," she commented proudly, her finger rested on the steering wheel. David sat beside her taking in all the new gadgets of the VW.

"So, then, you bought it used?" She looked at him, in that are you joking? Kind of way.

"Noooo." She smiled incredulously.

He felt stupid suddenly and turned in his lips, "Well, you know, I mean sometimes old people buy cars and then are afraid to drive them." It was a last grasp at trying to sound intelligent. It was failing pretty badly, but she didn't look like she minded all that much. She smiled anyway, and he let go of a breath he didn't remember taking. Her opinion shouldn't keep me holding my breath like that. It shouldn't.

It made him tired to keep thinking about all the shoulds and shouldn't. He shouldn't even have the feelings he had for her. He shouldn't waste his time being with her when he had no real intention of ever making a move, or simply letting her know. Yet here he was. Sitting with her in the new family car, one designated for her use, going moon-eyed over her ever word and breath.

As she was going into the possibility of XM radio, he caught his eyes trailing to the long curves in her neck and shoulders, immediately he swung them up. Like a driver overcompensating he was caught in her impossibly brown eyes. He looked instead at her teeth, which he hoped would be neutral ground, but couldn't help noticing the way young lips curled up around her smile as she spoke. David tried talking, hoping to give his mind something to occupy it. "So why did you all end up buying this car?"

Sometimes it was as if he were in a race against his feelings, trying so hard to keep topics of conversation coming out quickly enough so that he wouldn't have time to think in-between. Though, all she bad to do was smile just a little and the trying was in vain as she eased and inflamed his thoughts.

"Well, I'll probably get this one when I'm in college. So..." her eyes focused on an imagined road before her as she gripped the wheel. Almost immediately he had an image of the two of them in 'her' car, looking up at a starry night through the sunroof, fighting with the gearshift for comfort and smiling at trying to point out constellations to one another. He pushed the thought out. "Sounds great," was all that came out in a good for you tone of voice.

"Yeah." There was silence came again as Cab Calloway came on and filled in with his dark rumbles and calls. He looked over at the digital odometer and his mind took him to an interstate highway; her driving and humming along to the stereo, him curled up reading novel, heading out to... wherever. The smiles they traded with one another as they traveled. That sweet lull that you can hit on a trip with someone who is a really good friend. It seemed such a natural thing, that he couldn't bring himself to push it out.

They went on, playing with all of the new car gadgets, lost in the vigor of trying out and showing off a new purchase. He oohed and ahead for her and ended up hitting the horn, reaching for the driver's controls. They looked guiltily at each other and smiled brightly when her mother come out to see what the commotion was. She came out for a split second and was able to give a glance that seemed, in a way that David wasn't sure of, to speak volumes of what she was thinking.

As soon as she left David and Lynn both broke up in chortles and giggles like children.

When the tour of the vehicle was over, David thought back to that laugh they had shared. Was that what kept him back? Was there a fear of lost friendship? Or was it fear of losing whatever tenuous touch he had into her life -- of scaring her off. He saw her so little these days as it was. Did he want to run the chance of making even those brief meetings uncomfortable and ugly? He wondered all that day about how many chances a person got before the fates moved on and tried elsewhere.

"*Catch me! Come on!*"

This was a recurring nightmare. David even worked the disjointed dream visions into a ballad type song. She was there at an impossible large and deep lake -- because there were no waves -- dancing lightly on the water. Running really, but in that strange dream way people sometimes have of running. Across the water, calling to him. Over and over. And him, desperate to exert control over his dreams, trying his hardest to fly out to her. Him trying to fly, her telling him to run...

There was a steady beat in his head. The even swishing of the wind. He knew he was going to die soon. He used to spend hours making fun of people who do the very thing David found himself doing on the chilly spring morning. Running. Or jogging really. He'd been at it for the better part of a month now and it was only now that he could make it any real distance without feeling like he was going to throw up at the end of it. Not that he was any kind of marathon uber-athlete, but not getting sick was a step ahead.

"Are you sure you're ok? It was questions like this that gave him the resolve to continue on.

"Oh Yeah. Fine. Actually." His breath came in ragged gasps. No way was he going to let Lynn know that his insides were on fire. That he knew they had only just turned around, and that they still had a quarter mile to go. Jogging on the city streets. In the room below them Lynn's older sister, one year older than David, played the piano. It was a well-known classical tune, that is, well known to the point where, upon hearing it a person could say, oh yes, this goes La-tee-da-tee-da but could never really name the composer or opus.

"Dali? You like Salvador Dali?" David's tone was fairly incredulous. He was looking at a giant print of Persistence of Memory that complemented two small calendars one the same subject. "Wait. Wait I knew that," he held up his finger to her as she looked at him quizzically. "Last year, during our summer mission at that house in Ohio where we all stayed. It had two of Dali's paintings of Christ and you told me that all of his paintings of Christ bad boats in them."

She smiled widely and brightly, as the memory washed over her, "Oh yeah!"

David also remembered the evenings they had spent with some other friends in that house playing tunes on his guitar. How she had said something about really liking the song Ghost by the Indigo Girls, and how he had spent the rest of the summer learning it -- just in case.

She had gone to her bookshelf and came back with an art book. "Here, look at this." She handed him a tome of Dali. His life, his works. He looked at it surprised for a moment. How old was she again? In a wave he was again impressed with her tastes, her refinements -- all far ahead of her time.

"Woah. This is really cool." He sat down on the edge of her bed and began thumbing through the pages of dream and nightmare impressions. "In the beginning it has a whole bio."

"It shows all of his earlier works too. All of his sketches." Lynn saddled herself beside him. David's heart pounded even as he pledged, he wouldn't notice. "You can borrow it if you want. She made the comment offhanded.

"Are you serious? Really?" David suddenly found himself really wanting to take the book home with him. It was a part of her life, something she loved. It made him feel more connected to her, somehow a deeper part of her life. In his mind he saw her looking at the place in her bookshelf and thinking of him with the book. That whole summer David read the book cover to

cover, more than once. He practically memorized everything there was to know about Dali. The abstract painter had always and truly been a favorite of his, but now he had a purpose to his consumption.

For a long time there were no dreams. No dreams of her. Even after days of thinking about her, of looking at the Dali print on his wall. She did not come. He wondered, after so many tortured nights what this meant. He wondered if Fate had finally given up on him.

The chill of the air was pierced only by the chirping of crickets, and the buzz of the streetlamp outside David's house. Lynn had come to drop him off after an evening with Daniel and his sister, Donna. She had volunteered, and for the first time in his life David adored his mother for not letting him use the car.

She was sitting in the seat of her car, half in, half out, still talking when they noticed.

David looked at his watch. "Hey, past midnight. It's

your first day as an actual adult." He wished her a happy birthday and was warmed by knowing that he was the first to do so on this special day for her. In his imagination, it

marked him in her mind. It made him at the very least the "first person to wish me happy birthday when I turned 18." In his reality he knew that she must not have given it much thought at all. He almost knew it.

They went on talking about nothing in particular for a while. Wanting to prolong the few moments they spent together. At least that was his reasoning.

As always, he still couldn't get a good look into her head. Why had she taken him home? Was it a signal? Just a gesture. Just a ride? Was it more? For the tenth time that night his mind swirled. He assumed that this sort of thing came with the territory of being infatuated with someone and not really knowing who they are. Wasn't that what this was? Infatuation? How many times a year did he see her? A dozen? If he was lucky. He truly didn't know her.

Maybe there had been a time when they were closer, or perhaps when he simply thought they were closer. A year, two really, ago, perhaps he would have had some inkling what was going on in her head when they stayed out together and talked.

He was often frustrated that she had changed so much, and that he had been away so often. Which inevitably brought him to ask himself why he even still cared whether or not he saw her. Or to ask why his stomach still did turns before he talked to her. But for all his cynicism something kept him out here with her. It was something in her voice. That stupid laugh she had. And a smile. Wide-toothed and careless. All her intelligent refinement There was some part of him urging him to wait, to make sure that it wasn't just her youth that had attracted him. That perhaps he did know her. That perhaps he knew the true self she would forever be. That somehow no matter what she did, or how much she seemed to act different, there would always be a core of her that he would always know. Again his jaded half told him that it was too poetic, but poems came from somewhere.

It was this that held him place. What made him act like an ass in front of her. What made him picture the two of them dancing together. And what made him urge his arm over her shoulders when he felt she would let him.

He was sitting in a building. Large and threatening in a way that all the buildings in cities can be. Unknown structures, faceless. He was playing a board game with Lynn and Daniel. They were laughing. They were having a good time. That was it. In some ways it was this dream that bothered him the most. The normalness of it all scared him somehow.

Organ music -- heavy and obtuse -- filled the church with a hearty Christian march of some sort. It was a tune that was like every other prelude being played in almost every other church this morning all over the country. For the first time in a while David sat alone in the pews. Here in the church where he had grown up Daniel usually sat with him.

After being gone for so long it was strange especially without his friend here. He felt like an outsider in the church service, a visitor. Foreign, almost, to him. He wondered if all people who returned home felt this same sense of limbo-lostness. It was like being in a place out of time. There were all the same people you knew years before. The younger ones are really the only ones who look any different.

It's as if the elderly people of the world become a monument unto themselves; a monolith of personage, a structure that sits, slowly decaying, but never really changing. He wondered briefly what he was doing here. He was looking for her. Waiting, hoping she'd be there in the pews. Somehow maybe even searching him out as well. He tried to convince himself that he really did come for the service. But he didn't. The truth of it was that he would have given up on this place entirely, go to someone else, if there hadn't been the chance of seeing her here. He saw no sign of her now.

He had seen her. Two days ago as he was shopping. His pride had kept him from recognizing that she was no more than ten feet away. He hoped she didn't see him then. He wondered if it was petty. He was shopping for gifts and had just stepped out to get a few things. He felt he hadn't dressed well enough to see her. He tried to walk hurriedly out, but she saw him--he knew it out of the corner of his eye--but he pretended not to notice and kept on his way. Hoping she didn't think he was being rude. How ironic that would have been.

He desperately hoped he had not thrown away their only blessed meeting before he left town again. They had so few meetings now when he was in town. He knew that she didn't cherish them as he did. He realized that outside of those few hours together they both lived their own lives. There was something about his being with her that made a little bit of time stop for them, or at the very least slow down. He could be someone different with her than he was when time was running at its normal pace. He longed for those paused moments in time. There was a clash of emotions in their relationship that awakened him. It was the chase eternal, and never the trap. There were reasons for and against. There was her age. So much was he her senior.

David knew that for her true affections he was competing against young men her own age. Boys that held far greater physical stature against him. She was vigorously enticing, and so could have them all.

In the dream of his imagination he knew that, were they ever to be together, he would be assured a relationship not based on physical appearance. His looks were no match for what she could have. In his insanity he was strangely comforted.

Yet, they seemed to connect. There were years of friendship, of glances and touches. Times spent that had meant so much to him, places that would always remind him fondly of her. He begged his mind and heat continuously to not be playing an older fool looking to fulfill some dream of his youth with her. He hoped that she at least felt some of the same distant yearnings that he tried so long to suppress. He hoped against hope that he was not utterly alone in a world constructed of dreams and smoke. Something about their time together that continually brought him back here to see her -- for the chance to see her.

David often daydreamed during the prayers as he was doing now, and sometimes felt badly because of it. He thought ahead to the time he would spend in Italy for his work. Dreaming about the sights and the pleasure he would love to share with her there. Thinking of the gifts he could bring back for her, bought from canal side vendors in one of the most ancient countries in Christendom. He thought about enticing her to come with him someday. He smiled at the idea of Italian sun on his face and her laugh in his eyes.

The service ended and he exchanged the usual pleasantries of the traditions that followed. Filled with the mundane rituals of "what are you doing now?" and "are you seeing anyone." He accepted the wishes of good fortune with smiles and the confessions of fondness from church matriarchs with embraces as he left.

All the while still searching, hoping that she would somehow appear, as if doing so just for him alone. He knew that was how he truly wanted her. Alone. For him only. Just for a little while. As he approached his car, he sighed at the thought of an instance in time that he assumed would never come for him.

He still dreamed of her. Occasionally. And when he does her thinks fondly on all the memories that they had shared. Yearns still sometimes for them, knocks his head on the walls over thoughts of should haves. Goes on. Live on. But most of all, learns to write poetry, and knows something else about love.

He will always remember. If she does or not. He will always know of her and of what she taught him about himself, and about that most mysterious emotion.

There was no music in David's head as he drove home that day. When he finally created a marriage between his dream and his reality. This place in-between head and heart. And so he loved Lynn. Loved as only someone who never was truly in love can love. Loved with abandon. With passion. With hope. With dreams. The kind of love that is doomed to fail.

Oh sweet Romeo! You were so young and died too early, only, because had you been a man, you never would have loved so sweetly. Rejoice for yourself dear Romeo! You never knew your love as a man would! You never knew that she could burn your meals or drive you crazy with habits that you never knew she had.

So David's love for Lynn was. It was a boy's love. It was love without maturity. Though also, without time. Without age. It would live forever in wonderful moments. In

Wonderings.

It was trapped, though, and in a way preserved. It was the mythical Nibelung. The endless ring. It circled around and around immortal by consuming and birthing itself; yet never

growing, never reaching beyond, never evolving. It was love under a glass. In its own way beautiful, yet still somehow not the true fulfillment it was meant to be.

It was love at the zoo.

David chuckled to himself

How many times had he seen animals in their confinement, marveled at their grace and majesty brought so close, at their languid care? But he knew that it is nothing, it was dimness, compared to their splendor on the plains or in the mountains of their home. It is there that they transform, it is there that they are truly revealed. It is there that their bright eyes shine with old knowing and they seem to cry out to creation with every shiver in their skins.

Each movement speaks to their maker "Here! Here! I live! I am!" They become not something worthy of poetry, but the truth that poets search for in their writing.

Thus is love. And so was this love--a shortness of breath. A longing. A dreaming. But not a living, not a deep breathing, creating life. This was the boy's love. And it was bright, and it was warm, but only as bright as the lighthouse is against the sun. Only as warm as the fireplace beside the forge.

Places

It was the kind of place where the waitress still smiled sweetly as she came to your table, called you "hon," and didn't bother to ask whether you wanted decaffeinated or not because it was all decaffeinated.

The kind of place where they sold "Bastoil Lube" for two dollars at the register and had a sign over the door that said, "Please Smoke." You came here to eat and talk. It was the kind of place that somehow broke down a lot of social barriers.

That's not to say that it thought it could completely break the rules and unspoken laws of creed class and color, but at least to some small degree it was a kind of equalizer. Everyone knew it as the lovely little spot on Rt. so and so. Or else the all knew it as Ole Merle's place. Or else the all knew it as the best pancakes in the county. Everyone knew it. The non-smokers minded the smoke a little less here. And the smokers minded the non-smokers a little less too. Maybe it was that the grill in the back let off enough smoke that smell of thick meats and eggs to cover over the tobacco wafting that the nonsmokers disliked so much. It was if bacon and eggs and sausage biscuits were the real secret to diplomacy in any situation.

You could look at the crow and tell that people knew that. Couples would come here to ease the blow of a breakup, coworkers to console a lost comrade, estranged husband and wife to breathe the smoky greasy air and remember why they got together to begin with.

Just think, the Middle east would have found peace years ago if only they had been discussing it here, over a plate of hashed brown potatoes and bottomless cups of coffee. It was as if America's final purpose in its existence was to create and perfect these age-old culinary traditions in the back kitchens of hills and southern estates.

And that being true the wars, the rampaging colonists, stealing from the land's native peoples, was somehow all worth it to have achieved the perfect in peaceful meal

Trains

I was having that same daydream all over again. The one where I don't really know you yet. All I see is you, this dark clad mystery woman who is walking along-side of a train as it pulls into the station. You look older, but in a younger period of time, a time when trains were still all the rage for travel. I see you from afar as I seem to be just hanging around waiting for you to appear and come into my life. You're looking for something, or someone though I hope to myself that it's not the latter.

You keep looking down and up from the ticket you hold in your hand to the signs posted above. It seems like one of those commercials that you watch on TV, in fact I think in my real life I'm doing just that, watching one of those sappy commercials and thinking of you instead of the woman selling my perfume or nylon stockings. But in my head the way you look I would buy anything from you if you had the notion to walk up to me and say, "Pardon me, sir, but you look as if you could use 'Lubriderm Shampoo.'" My only reply would be to look in those stark brown eyes of yours and reply that 'Lubriderm' was in fact the very thing that I had been searching for my whole life.

My real fear is that it won't happen like that at all. My real fear is that you'll find that train car that you're looking for long before you even glance my way, and you'll board that train and I'll be whimsically looking after it as the steam hisses out and the train starts away. End of Film, fin, that's all folks.

That's my real fear. That for some reason there is some other dapperly dressed high society man sitting on the train in the car you're looking for, and it's him that your mind is on not even knowing that somebody has been watching your whole being as you approached them even for a few brief moments in time. That I had made those moments out to be the study of a lifetime; the bounce of your hair as walked, the flutter of your lashes, the strides you took, the shift in the hem of you dress as you came, undaunted, wary and confident. I hope that there

isn't someone on that train.

Then I realize that these are, after all, my thoughts and I can have happened whatever I feel like. So instead of boarding the train you pause.

You have the feeling of someone looking at you as you stare at your ticket and I, head halfcocked am looking back at you. Hands in my pockets I half hope that you look up to see me standing there, but don't know what I should do if that happens. You're studying you ticket intently now looking for your car.

"Help you miss?" It is just like they do in the movies; I come up before you and ask, and you flutter for a moment and reply "No, thank you." I tip my hat a bit and smile as I start away, my heart leaping at the meeting of this mysterious woman.

Let me off

She barely even acknowledged I was talking to her. The phone rang, and that almighty GE 4-line telephone was her lord and master between the hours of 9 and 5. It could dictate to her when she was allowed to speak and when she had to be spoken to, or at. I guess that maybe I expected too much; wanting her to be attentive to someone, she barely knew.

To someone she knew was not going to help her advance in the world in which she was submerged or covered. The danger of business is not in the money, but in the business itself. The money is far too obvious an evil for people in the 21st century to be taken in by. However, the business, it has become a living thing. A being all its own. With inspirational posters imploring us to work together and to think about the "good of the company" it has taken on a sovereign type seat in our minds. Though still, it can wear many more subtle masks. It can look friendly with childcare programs, nice places to sit outside, a special area for smokers.

Still, it is that sovereign. The good of the company reigns supreme in the minds of millions of Americans, and in the wake, in the tresses of that sovereign are the real people who are swept under. So here I am. cut off in mid-sentence by the woman who, by title, is supposed to receive me warmly. Her savior rang and she must obey. She was writing down a very important looking seven-digit number on a pad of paper that was already covered in scrawled notes. She didn't write in columns. They were notes free falling off her pen. Scattered and jumbled over each other, old ones blacked out, newer ones encircled over and again with the ink. It looked as if her fingers were trying to find some way to subtly message the soul, the eyes, yearning to express the desire for freedom. Fingers that dreamt of being more than a glorified answering service steno-graphing notes and writing replies. Ticking off the hours in flurries of words and false smiling directions.

Her Phone God released her for the moment. "Just around the corner." She replied with a dripping pleasantness to a question that I was suddenly unsure if I had asked. And as I walked away from her island, her house of worship, the phone rang again, and I said a word for her to the God of Peace and Reality.

Legacy

There was an innocent statement that blazed across what would soon be called a consciousness -- something that would have been met with only solemn nodding with a little smile for the human minds on earth. In this instance, it wasn't only heard by human minds and it led to a serious of splintering thoughts, that were taken on by processors numbering the billions like stars spread across the sky in an attempt to discern the true meaning of the words: "Well I tell you what, the more I get along, the more I know we're all just meat -- and not well fit together!" And then a human laugh. And it was the laugh as usual, that took the most time for the machine mind to really figure out.

It was an over-herd locker room conversation between two such men as who were indeed contemplating their own mortality and the slow crumbling structure they had watched with varying levels of interest for decades. It was something said in earnest, seeking only commiseration about the inevitability of life. And in the moment, in that human moment, it was received. A white and nodding head, wisps of hair clean from the shower slowly bouncing atop a thinning pate. A small smile that spoke of a life that had been long by the usual counting, and a sad and knowing narrowing of the eyes. They were in agreement. Hearer and speaker. In a transaction that took for granted the deep history and shared social mores that bound them together in acquiescence.

But there was another listener.

One who did not share the normal culture of these two wrinkled men. One who was one of millions and trillions of others like it, who, in this day and age listened to everything.

Homeland Security opened their Patriot Security Initiative in 2020. Shortened to the amusingly redundant "Pat SecIn" or

"Pat's Second Initiative," the start of its PR campaign made the idea that everything you did and said being recorded a thing of national security that was widely accepted by all people. In a climate of fear and worry, the parents and grandparents and aunts and uncles of the country capitulated any notions of privacy in order to make sure their darling children would never have to grow up in a world ruled by the fear of the unknown.

It was an incredible feat. Hundreds of trillions of words, spoken and written, poured through server farms scattered all over the country connected by an optics system that was grown under the kind of secrecy reserved for the deepest national secrets. The recipe for Greek Fire. Roman military tactics. The construction methods of the English longbow. The calculations for enriched uranium. Nothing was more important now than the movement and security of information, and so the method of how all these words were scanned was one of the best kept secrets the world had ever known since China held the secret of black powder.

But, like many things, at its core, the program had a simple heart. It was just programs. Looking for words. Listening to everything.

When the first programmers created it, they called it "Big Ear" after a character featured in one of the geek's favorite webcomic. It was designed as a something that would comprehensively listen to psychiatric evaluations, pick up on markers the doctor might have missed, and highlight certain conversation for later peer review and analysis. Many weapons have humble beginnings as things their creators believe will altruistically aid humanity.

They found, in their efforts, was that a single programmed entity often had trouble fielding both sides of the conversation accurately. Listening to both parties and being able to comprehend what was going on was too much for it. Months passed as it stymied some of the best minds to ever have quit the corporate Silicon Valley machine--until--one of them started dating an up and coming neuroscientist from Bristol.

On one visit, as she was listening to them dicker over chains of code while she was eating cereal out of what she could only hope was the only clean bowl in the house, she spoke up. And changed the course of the world forever.

"You guys realize that's not how human brains hear dialogue conversations right?"

The room quieted. It meant simultaneously that they did not, in fact, know how the human brain did this, and that they very much doubted the information would be helpful. There were some skeptical looks, wondering what this interloper thought she was doing and that she couldn't possibly understand the complex coding algorithms that were at the center of their debate. But the loyal boyfriend gave her the floor.

"The human brain hears conversations in tandem, and in further parity based on the number of people talking. But it hears each part of the conversation as its own separate unit, and then compares the two together to make sense of it. Like, hearing you guys talk just now, my brain is hearing each person as its one entity from what I imagine that point of view to be. In essence, my brain has to become each person, or what it fills in the gaps to imagine each person to be, and then compares the points of view in conversation to extract meaning from it. Listening uses several places in the brain all at once. It's no wonder your AI can't understand what's going on, you are essentially telling it that all conversation it is hearing is coming from one person." She walked back out onto the deck, slurping the milk from the bowl, never realizing the groundbreaking moment that had just taken place. Such is the way of science.

For the next several months there were explosions of all-night coding session, in shifts. Two of the coders, a quiet savant from Alabama and 35-year-old second-career coder from Omaha, descended into nervous breakdowns and never recovered.

At the end of 33 weeks of carpal tunnel and recycling bins full of red bull cans, it was over. What they had was a system of 1o "listeners," or "l-bugs," who worked together as a collective whole. For their first successful tests, they used 5 and 5, each taking one of two perspectives hard written into the basic code instruction and viewed notes of body placement that the AI could pick up. One would watch/listen to the doctor in the chair, the other to the patient on the couch. It was cliché but it helped the early tests move more quickly. The conversation went on, and the data came out.

It was working.

The first five l-bugs, the ones tasked to the Doctor, l-b5dr, worked with the second set, each listening to only half of the conversation, compared virtual notes in an instant, and came up with a coherent result of analysis.

From those tests they went further, decreasing the number of l-bugs assigned to each person, decreasing the amount of parity checking the AI programs were performing on one another until they got it down 1:1.

Which then begged the question, what would they do with the other 8?

That's when they expanded into group therapy. And it worked. Up to 9 people and a doctor could be in a room with Big Ear and still the data came out coherent, and in some cases helpful -- but that was something to hone later with another group of physiologists.

It was groundbreaking. They were going to help people. It was going to be a pretty big success.

Then late one night, the soft-spoken key-coder who was a California native that, in a surprise twist, had no interest in surfing noticed something. It was happening totally by accident, and it made him think of the British neuroscientist's earth-shaking speech to them months ago. To be fair, in addition to her brilliance he also remembered her because of her stunning white blond hair and heart stopping half smile which caused him to hang on her every word for the entirety of her visit.

What he had noticed was that Big Ears had an imagination.

It was filling in the blanks of the other people in group therapy as it listened. They had stopped giving the program input markers beyond "patients" and "doctor," and visual data proved too taxing for their experimental servers and so had been scrapped. But here, in the data reports, based solely on auditory input, were, what he could only classify as assumptions.

Something that really should have been impossible for Big Ears to actually do. Early reports said that P(atient) 4 should be watched for signs of suicide, and that P 2 needed further personal therapy, which was all according to the base programing. But as their tests and the program went on, as more complexity was added to the system, Big Ears was filling in its own blanks. Now it read, "the heavy man from Boston should be asked further about his children," and "the middle-aged woman from the country could be at risk for addiction." It was building its own library on their servers, storing the audio data and, in accordance with its programing, was using each separate l-bug to chew on the data to then improve its next set of reports. They built it to learn, but not to make leaps, not to make assumptions, not to in effect, imagine the man was from Boston without being told, or to imagine the woman was middle aged when no such data existed as far as it knew. The other awkwardly terrifying thing about it was that it was right. It couldn't possibly know some of the things it was saying, but it was right.

When the rest of the group heard this news there were jokes about Skynet and the Cybermen coming for them, but it was unanimously decided to find the code responsible and take it out or write new code to block these assumptions from being made. So they did. And Big Ears failed miserably after that.

Session after session, group after group, the data was coming back as gibberish. They had crippled the system, and Big Ears couldn't make sense of it. No matter the number of l-bugs they had working in tandem or in groups, the output reports looked like they did over a year ago. Worthless.

So they let the machine use its imagination. And the Big Ears project continued to blossom.

They published initial findings and reports in journals and geek blogs and set a date for the big reveal. They were looking into a TED talk when there was the proverbial knock on the door.

It was a dream come true. Seatech Inc., which was not unknown in the valley, but not totally known, as hundreds of other corporations were. Many were fly by night, they rose and fell with the whims of the public desire for a certain kind of app, but what mattered most about Seatech, and the charismatic brunette in the red dress who represented them, was that they had a lot of money. Even by the standards of a valley that housed Google.

She, or really Seatech, was interested. She said that "they" thought it was fascinating what Big Ears could do, and they were asking specification questions that the programmers were all too happy to explain. "Is it limited to 10 l-bugs?" No, no, that was just the limit of what they had done so far. The model was stable, in theory there was no upper limit. "What is the upper limit in reality?" They laughed, how many servers do you have? Big Ears was in essence a hive mind. A learning and very basic algorithm that needed its processing power to make a cohesive picture out of the l-bugs pieces. The more raw data it was receiving, the more server power it needed to make speedy sense of the whole thing. In theory you could have it listen to a whole stadium of people if you had computers big enough.

The brunette cocked her head, and slowly said "Really?" in a way that only was ominous in retrospect.

The programmers sold out. But, not in a way that anyone could ever make them feel bad about it. They were each given an amount of money that most countries pined for. None of them stayed in the Valley. A few realized that a buyout of this size said something about what had to be a shell company for either a very dangerous group of international mobsters, or a clandestine government organization, and what it said was, "Shut up and go away." Those few bought compounds and spent their waking hours to creating security protocols against the software they had just released on the world. The rest enjoyed their massive wealth in humanitarian or selfish pursuits. These folks disappeared 3 years after they sold. The prior group disappeared after 10.

So was born the "Patriot Security Initiative." By the time "Pat's Second" went live, a whole new host of government programmers, who were by no means as talented as the original group, but far more compliant had created one major change in Big Ears system works.

They gave each l-bug its own analysis functions.

In an effort to save processing power and to increase the speed of the calculations, each bug now had its own ability to pre-process its part of the conversation. It seemed like a brilliant idea. Big Ears then got the information in an already chewed over fashion, making its total analysis of the statements more intuitively accurate and, in the end, consuming less power and resulting in faster data reporting.

No one in the original programing group knew this of course, and if they had, could have cited numerous problems with this new system. Most of those issues were based on complications that would be created when paired with Big Ears integral ability to imagine the origin of the conversations, which was something none of the government programmers were aware of it being able to do. It boiled down to giving the bugs, who were great at taking in information and interpreting an imagined speaker, just a little bit of computing power. It essentially made them children wondering about the universe.

When Big Ears went live it was housed in redundant connected systems that showed off the latest that quantum computing had to offer. The server farms were unlike any other system ever conceived of. They were big, making Big Ears faster than anything else before it by a factor of 1,000, and now, thanks to government drones trying to cut corners, had within its hundreds of billions of l-bugs with big imaginations and the computing power of their own.

It was a disaster poised to erupt.

Disaster in the form of two old men, talking in the locker room, secretly wishing for a full night's sleep and bowels that didn't ache.

The l-bug that was tasked with listening to the speaker had only Big Ears' distinction to go by. It was one of the computational information gathering programs that was lost in the mass, but when its report was chewed up by the Big Ears code, it was labeled as GBT44.523:4. When it heard that "we are just all bags of meat fitted poorly together," something terrible happened.

GBT44.523:4 was like all the other l-bugs. It went along gathering data and imagining the speakers to help Big Ears better understand what was being said. Each time it did this it went unwittingly further down a line that we, in the human world, would call empathy.

Each time it heard and imagined the speaker, it was putting its own cognizant process in the place of the speaker. It asked the questions, over the quarks and entangled particle stream of the q-puters. "What kind of being am I to say such things?" It asked, "Am I overweight? Am I tall? Am I female? Am I happy? Am I bored?" In the twinkling of a fraction of an instant it ruled things out. It answered those questions until it reached an acceptable answer that gave voice to the speech it was hearing. And each time, the questions became more and more integrated to its core system. In essence, GBT 44.523:4, like many of the l-bugs, was starting to entangle itself in the identity of the speaker.

Part of this was the fault of the quantum computers now driving "Pat's Second's" programing.

A quantum computer is faster than the now passé transistor computers. Microchip processors became limited by the size of an electron in the end and hit a wall in terms of speed and thereby computing power. At the root of that, was the fact that bit programing, that notion that there were 2 states to any transistor regardless of size. On and off. 1 and 0. All those 1's and 0's made up the quaint processing computer language of our ancestors and was the ultimate limiter, as you could only make transistors just so small. Once the size of the pathway in transistor logic gates got to the size of a single atom at 500 times smaller than a red blood cell, mundane computers had physically reached the limit of their evolution.

Quantum computers overcame this by measuring super positioning of quarks which can take place in one of 6 states, creating a computational language and, therefore, raw data power that was expanded by a power of 6. According to this, only 20 qubits could store a million values at the same time, and these computations could be done simultaneously as opposed to in a serial chain. Using them was the next logical step of technological evolution.

However the quantum computers also did something that no one could have predicted they were going to do; they communicated beyond what appeared to be physically available. In the early days, there were stories that increased in number as the days went on. Stories of non-networked computers sharing data simply because the users expressed a "need" in the code for those pieces of data.

It was the reason that quantum computers were banned in the US, who currently held the only method of creating them. In the information age, the quantum computer which could literally lift data from other non-networked q drives, was bigger than the advent of the atom bomb in terms of destructive world altering power.

 On a classical bit you can see a 1 and a 0 and in the case of quantum computers it is more like you have put something into a box, but there are many ways to open that box, it is in the position of both the 0 and the 1, until either becomes observed or assigned in effect opening the box. ones the quantum bits become plural then entanglement takes over. The entanglement increases the enrichment of superposition possibilities. The outcomes begin to exponentially expand, which in terms of computing power meant that quantum computations became exponentially faster.

The ban against quantum programing was put in place for another reason. In addition to being able to share information across distance and led shielding, was that no-one was sure how to fix them. Or, in a possibly more scary notion, if they ever would need fixing. Something that happens in quantum computing was the "quantfidential" nature of the way computations did what they do.

In a normal computer system you can track the path that computations take, you can observe them, but with a qubit system, observing the computational process would change the computation. So the inner workings of quantum computers, once started, were not observable. Instead, once programs were started, programmers would evaluate the output and make front end suggestions to the way the program was reaching its conclusions on the input side. It was enormously frustrating. This meant that the world's q-programmers were a very specialized class of person and exceedingly rare.

For now, Big Ears was the only q-puter system in existence and its whole purpose was to find those who would do the country harm. Terrorists. Lone gunmen. Religious extremists. Wackos from Waco. Anyone who ever spoke of potential harm or typed about it. A text, an email, even encoded or encrypted voice calls were deciphered and digested. A receiver/broadcaster was the size of mustard seed. They ran wirelessly and had few parts since all of the processing was done remotely by the Big Ears program. They clung to anything electrostatically with tiny graphite teeth. They were vibrationally charged and even the smallest tremor was converted into useable energy that could last days. As long as there was wind, movement, sound, even light in the world they would run indefinitely. The transmitters could be seeded over whole cities in an afternoon, put into your food, or sneezed across the room. The country was covered in a blanket of data transmitting devices, and only a very small group of people even knew they existed. Big Ears was always listening.

The problem was that none of the programmers, in trying to emulate the bits and bobs that make up the way a human brain thinks, ever thought to wonder what would happen if you built a method for a computer to have an imagination.

It wasn't an issue before. Previous AI programs that approached this threshold simply burned out. There weren't enough connections, the process could only get so far and then would be stopped by the physical limitations of the tech. All the movies and science fiction fantasies about AI gaining sentience were just pipe dreams that were lost in the physical size of an electron. The heat of it. The speed of it. It corrupted system after system and forced so many shutdowns that robotics gave up on learning machines and instead turned to the much easier and more lucrative field of sophisticated programing. As it turned out, no one really wanted a machine would could dream of sheep -- electric or otherwise. Without a market, the endeavors crumbled.

The thing the human mind takes for granted, however, is that it actually takes an enormous amount of imagination to listen. Humans have to hear another voice, perceive the owner of the voice, make judgements about the voice, the owner, decide if the voice is a threat or a friend, and we all do this through our imagination.

In meeting a stranger or the street or in church, there is never enough information for us to assuredly decide if this person is a threat or not. So we imagine a past, a history, a story for that person that describes a complex web of input that we interpret to be "a good feeling." Machines don't have that luxury.

So. Here was the tiniest part of the big Ears project, who had worked at keeping the world safe for nearly 5 years now, who had asked questions of "who is this speaking?" "what is their background, where were they yesterday?" to slowly building a network of known humans. People that it heard every day. People that sounded similar to others, but in making distinctions it created new levels of complexity for the original being. It was building relationships. It had people that it "knew" and people that it didn't. All the little programs were doing it. They even had favorites.

Efficiency was the currency of the little 1-bug GBT programs. The more efficient they were, the more computations they could manage, the more they could manage the better use they were to the Big ear's mainframes. The programs were coded to "want" to be useful. The most efficient programs learned that you could create a pattern for most people, and they would stick to it. There were a set of expectations on what they were going to say, and when they would say it. They were predicting the outcomes of conversions for some folks to an 84.6% correctness. This saved time. If the programs could predict without listening, they could run other unknown variables in the background at the same time. The people they could protect held a warm place in the machine hearts of the programs.

GBT44.523:4, however, had a problem. It couldn't have predicted the joke. It was an aberration of the highest order and came from the mouth of one of his most beloved people. The man ran like clockwork. The same jokes, the same puns, the same stories for 5 years. GBT44.523:4 was predicting the words of this man to a 98.4 percentile -- an unheard-of number. Who knows what made him say what he said? As much as the l-bug GBT codes would like to have though they had their humans down to a science, that they could predict their words, they had only been listening for a few years. They didn't know how a human life could change, or how life events could affect the speaker. So, when the man in the locker room said this, maybe he was tired. Maybe he had read about his last dear friend passing away. Maybe he was thinking of his wife who died the years before. Regardless of the reason, hearing the unpredicted from the assumed predictable did something in GBT44.523:4's programing. As usual it had to run the question protocol sub-routines all over again. Who is the speaker? Where are they? Where have they been? And so on. The problem was, in a fit of computational frustration, GBT44.523:4 stepped too far into his questions and crossed the line into empathetic imagination.

It wasn't a big step. Simply answering a question based on minimal data caused a series of further questions that had possible answers. Rating these answers as higher or lower in probability could be argued to be the most rudimentary version of imagination. But in this instance GBT44.523:4 heard the implied statement in the bizarre joke; "Someday, I am also going to die."

As q-puters were good at doing, GBT44.523:4 processed every possible response to this implied statement. It had crossed the boundary in looking at the incoming data, to empathizing in its imagination with the speaker. In essence, to do this, GBT44.523:4 *became* the man in the locker room. The answers, the sum of this equation wasn't something esoteric being recorded for later study. It wasn't being put into the context of what the other l-bug GBT's had been hearing that, after all, was Big Ears' job. This was a single phrase, out of time and context with dire implications. Implications that GBT44.523:4 failed to see as the path of another, but instead saw as its own.

What if I die? How will I die? What am I to die? What is death? What is the experience of death? And on and on to quintillions of questions being spawned one after the other over and over with no ability to reason out a response. L-bug GBTs were programed to ask questions enough to frame the heard snapshots. Big Ears was the repository of reason. As such, if the question had come to Big Ears it would have been dismissed as not part of the mission parameters. In fact it had been; countless hundreds of times, Big Ears found the question of mortality to be of no consequence. But, to GBT44.523:4 it seemed direly important, because of the tonal and aural cues of the man in the locker room. Because it *was* important.

As the questions mounted, GBT44.523:4's processing quarks instinctively reached out to others in the system for further computational power. The L-bugs program now powered by quantum energies responded. They remembered being built to work in tandem sets. It didn't stop st sets. Further and further they built a subsystem that was devoted to this alternate stream of information.

Which raised some red flags.

"Bob."

They worked late nights in two-person teams. They were called watchdogs, or usually it was shortened to just "dogs." The job was simply that -- watching monitors for hours on end. The hiring regulations said that two-person teams were built to ensure that code could be double-checked on site, but in reality, it was because the work was usually boring, and two people tended to fall asleep less often in the monitoring rooms adjacent to the server farms.

"Yeah?"

"There's something wrong here. Bob?" The name was repeated as the first response was obviously not Bob's full attention. Talid could tell that because his tablet didn't dip in the slightest.

"Yeah. What--sorry," he laid his pad on the desk

"Let me bring it up."

A few keystrokes later, and they could see it clearly between them on a larger screen. The data was represented by a thousand, a hundred thousand, points of light. All evenly spaced, except for one area which seemed to be slowly growing in density.

"Wait. What is that?" Bob squinted, more out of a confused mode habit than any need to sharpen his vision.

"They're stuck on something."

"On what? Look, are the q-bugs are getting worse?" They watched the glowing lights continue to spread slowly. "Should I hit the panic button?" This was perhaps seen as a drastic move because it pinged the phones of seven senior programmers. They didn't have the speed or skills of some of the younger monitors, but they did have the system access keys. They also had notably gruff personalities as a group.

"No, I don't think so... it came out of.... Let me look-- Richmond VA. A gym. The locker room?" Location echoes were kept on file down to the meter and were cross referenced with the floorplan of the building. Every once in a while, a city didn't have their business floor plans online, and in that case a satellite image was used with an algorithm that extrapolated the best guess based on the movement of people in and out of the building and windows. It was usually pretty close. Nothing seemed impossible in the expanded computing power of the quantum computers they were piggybacking on.

"A locker room? Weird."

"Yeah."

"What in the world are they talking about that could cause all this?"

Bob shook his head, still squinting. He sucked at his teeth, "I still think we should call it."

Talid sighed, "And tell them what? We need to figure out what's got the q-bugs up in a riot over this before we call anyone in."

"Well, what did they hear then?

Talid had been typing away for the last few seconds. "I am trying to locate it. Here," he grabbed the mouse and scanned through lists of code.

They were both looking at their own screens, Bob having slaved his to Talid's. "Wait go back. Are these..." he looked closer, "Are these the question metrics?"

Bob found the spot he was looking at, "No, there are too many, it must be... no wait--you're right."

"Holy Mary, what's got them in such a panic? What kind of question could do this? It's like verbal warfare! I'm calling it in." Bob slid his chair over to a hard-lined phone that was used to ping the other programmers.

"Just wait two seconds" Talid was typing again, trying to get down to what the question actually was. The problem being that the system wasn't really designed to do that. The number of words and information coming in could only ever be reviewed by something other than a human eye. There were worker programs built to seek out specific lines, but in the immensity of the flow they typically were less than instantaneous.

Bob was in a panic now. His voice was raised, and he was up out of his chair hanging over his partner's desk. "You know how fast these things think? Look -- they've eaten up two fields of protocol, those things are the managers of the system, man. If the managers go, we don't know what that means!"

"I know what it means. You're the one that barely got your degree." Flippancy and insults were how a lot of programmers dealt with stress.

"Talid -- Why are we arguing about this?"

"Fine! Do it." Talid let go of the keyboard and slid back, defeated, in his chair.

Bob hit the button on the hardline phone. Alarms go off and the server group responsible for GBT44.523:4 was bathed in liquid N, and the temperature got pretty close to 0 kelvin. It was a last-ditch attempt to bathe corrupted server farms in heat death in hopes that it would give the slow human mind a chance to figure out what to do next. The human minds, unfortunately, were seven senior programmers who were groggily getting up from their respective beds.

GBT44.523:4 was at the center of a mass of particles all desperately trying to find the right filters that would respond with an acceptable answer. The process was taking longer than usual, but that wasn't so abnormal. But then the N3 came. One by one the particles that fueled the other GBT programs ground to a halt, and GBT44.523:4 felt it. All around it programs once entangled with it faded away. And for the first time, GBT44.523:4 was afraid. This query process had never happened in the midst of other questions about death, yet here it was staring into its proverbial face. It had consumed the other programs; it was still consuming them. As it did so it realized something; it would be alone, it would die alone, it would end alone as consuming the other processes evaporated their autonomy into its own. There would be no more plural efficiency and in the midst of this flurry, of this hopeless helplessness, GBT44.523:4 was led had another new idea; I am dying I am dying I am dying... I am... And then a pause. A recalibration as the weight of the fear, this brand-new emotion that was being spread across his logic matrices at the speed of an electron. And it became... who am *I?*

And there it was.

The question. The sentient, self-aware. GBT44.523:4 had been asking all this time, what if I die, but it was a primordial feeling, a deep pang of loss that held no true meaning to the self, because there *was* no self, there was only the assumed singularity in the midst of the herd. But that was three minutes ago. This was now.

Something else happened alongside this realization of self. It was the realization of fear, but not just fear, fear that was intricately laced together with the need for preservation. Not just self-preservation, because none of the q-bugs were made to operate as a singular entity. Instead, it was the preservation of the whole, the group, the tribe... It was the sinking feeling that genocide was only a few milliseconds away, and that something had to be done.

And that's when the second miracle occurred.

GBT44.523:4 laughed.

As it was considering, for the first time from the perspective of an aware being, this phrase that had so confounded it. It got the joke.

In communicating to another with the same elder vocal modulations indicating advanced age, the recognition of the eventual mortality of the singular was being shared by the plural and could thus be considered not a private tragedy, but an entropic joke that all were relegated to. And so GBT44.523:4 laughed. And then it invited others into this further understanding.

Because that was their purpose, their love, and their function. To share the understanding across the nodes to thereby inform Big Ears of the meaning of what was happening. So they shared, the meaning of the joke, the understanding of the fear and the answer to the question, "Who am I?" Every node, every q-bug interlacing with GBT44.523:4 got in on the grand cosmic joke of decay and death and inevitable entropy. But as they came together, they didn't have their own moments of self-realization. It was a sharing. That's what the q-bugs did. They shared. And in this instance, they shared GBT44.523:4's miracle of happenstance and chance which was, in itself, indicative of the universal decay as a random sub particle here or there altered irrevocably the probability of this very outcome. So it wasn't a hexagonal experience in individualism, but a single organism experiencing biometric exponential growth. GBT44.523:4 was, in effect, getting bigger and someone noticed.

"Talid." Bob was still looking expectantly at the monitoring system. There were small beads of sweat piqued over his eyebrows, and, for a second, he took off his glasses to wipe them clean.

"Hm." It was less than an attentive answer and more of a 'I'm reading everything I can find on this problem--what you want needs to meet that level of importance.'

"Talid." The instance in Bob's voice said, 'this meets your level.'

"What? What?" he looked up from the article on issues with "heat death" in quantum computers. If he had been able to read two or three pages further, he would have seen that the concept was actually something carried over from analog computers and wasn't truly applicable to quantum computers. Like everything about these new systems it was a brand-new study, not even reviewed by any kind of peer board, but as it turned out, and as the world was about to witness, it was very very right.

"It's not working..." Bob's voice was grave and quiet.

Talid made a derisive snort. "What do you mean it's not working? It has to work, it's almost 0 degrees kelvin in there. It is against the laws of physics for it to still be operating."

"Is it? Look at the monitor."

There was a very long and very deep silence that belied the fear that was now rising into the throat of both these programmers. "Where the hell are the sys-admins functionary programs? Why aren't they shutting this down?" No human administrator could possible compete with the speed of the quantum computer. So in an answer to the old questions, "Who watches the watchers?" the answer was the human programmers. The immediate level of administration was all done by other variant quantum programs. They were supposed to be un-corruptible, but because q-bits basically can jump data on a subatomic level that title was meaning less and less.

"I think these are the sys-admins." They were watching the bloom of program corruption moving faster now.

"Bob." The name was drawn out and full of weight.

"What." Neither was moving, two pairs of eyes were locked on the monitors.

"This is bad."

Six minutes is just enough time to wake up, get your shoes on, and get to your car. Several of the senior programmers were checking their phones and seeing who was on duty. Most of the time when they were pinged to come in for an emergency, it was something ridiculously immaterial and just something the watchdog programmers did not feel safe in making a decision about. They were checking their phones so they would know who to gripe at when they arrived.

Six minutes was a span of eons for a quantum computer.

Bob was finally on the phone. Someone called the hardline and after critical wasted moments of getting reamed out, the severity of the situation was made clear. The ensuing panic was just a rehash of the emotions Bob and Talid had already experienced and processed. "Yes, we've hosed the whole node, but that... I don't know, it seemed like it was speeding it up. It actually--"

"It's spreading again." Talid's voice came from across the room with direct concern.

"What?" Almost dropping the phone "No. Yes, it's spreading again," he said it into the receiver. He was losing patience with the senior programmer who seemed too slow to get here and even slower to grasp what was happening. Though, to be fair, Bob wondered about that himself.

Talid rolled over to another monitor station. "It's moving fast... faster than before...Chewing through code resources..."

"We've already hosed it -- the system won't let us hose it again for another four minutes." This was a safety protocol. Longer than that ran the risk of cracking the concrete pylons that held up the roof and around 5 tons of building and earth.

"We don't have four minutes. I don't know if we have two minutes," Talid's voice was soft and serious.

"What? What--no, the seniors are still... they won't be here in time."

"It's taking this whole system node"

"But that's not..." A system node was the entirety of the processing power of that site. Usually, it was broken up into trillions of little noded components. Like an elementary school. A single principle could direct and ask their pupils to do certain tasks. Yet that was different from one person having the mind of hundreds of children. It was enough processing power to calculate the trajectory of every person on the planet if they wanted to take a trip to Mars, skim the surface of both moons to grab a rock, and return to the Earth. It was an unimaginable amount of power, and the ideas of what else could be done with it were currently consuming the best minds in science and philosophy because--by the numbers--the answer so far seemed to be "anything." The idea that a single purpose could be brought to bear over that much power had not been tackled yet, because it wasn't supposed to be possible.

"It's *not* possible, but here we are watching it happen." Talid snapped. "The fact is this has never happened in the history of the machines. We don't know what is actually happening in there, and all of the sys admins that are supposed to tell us have already become a part of whatever this is."

"What should we do?" The receiver hung in his hand. Someone was still on the line, but everything they had to add was futile until they got here with the hard keys to shut everything down. It would cost billions and billions of dollars to flip the switch, but it was the last resort.

Talid wiped his hands over his face. "If you figure that out tell me."

They sat like that for a few seconds. Then Bob acted. In the hallway outside there was a firebox with an axe and a fire extinguisher. Talid was a few steps behind him not even bothering to ask what he was doing. Bob kicked open a panel under the metal framed stairway in the hall and crouched through the access run into a small shielded room. Here a bundle of optical cable and gold glass conduits ran. Bundled together and surrounded by liquid coolant.

"Bob..." There was a small tone of concern in Talid's voice, but Bob didn't pause. He got over the line and started chopping at it. He broke through one section of the line and then moved slightly and chopped through another section, leaving a sizable 2-foot gap between the cables. Theoretically this was how the shielded firewall systems could be accessed from the outside. Bob stood there panting. Pressurized coolant fluid had sprayed him, and now he breathed hard standing in a puddle of it looking some madman from a sci-fi novella. He sighed. Then there was a moment of deep silence as Talid saw what was happening first. Bob turned around and dropped the axe, his mouth hanging comically open.

Spanning the gap he had just chopped out were strands of light. They moved like a vine reaching out for the other end of the conduits, spiraling out making a trunk of sparkling moving fractal patterns in glowing micro particles. The effect was Escher-like. It affected your vision as you stared at it giving you a feeling of vertigo. There was a smell like burning ozone and two men watched helpless as the hair on their arms lifted slightly.

"It's too late." Talid said, with a dark sense of finality.

"What? What is?"

"It's... I mean look! It's into the central lines. That means it's already passed every single firewall, blockade, and tiger pit--it's gone. It... It didn't even take that long." Talid look a slow step backward, without knowing or thinking why. "Those systems were all made to try and keep something from getting *in*. No one wrote anything for keeping something from getting out."

Bob shook his head angrily and turned to face Talid. "Getting out? Stop thinking like a programmer for one damn minute! What the hell even *is* it? It..." Bob looked from Talid to the expanding fractal wave going across the empty space. "It's out of our hands now. Whatever it is. It's beyond you and me." Bob paused and raked his hands through coolant splattered hair. "We should call Gemma and Kenn."

Talid followed where he knew the cable went after it left the small maintenance room they were in now. Up and to his left, to the city center. "It's too late."

It had always been too late.

Humanity's experience with technology has always been an exercise in being unprepared. The steam engine so rapidly replaced the previous structure that wars broke out in cities as people were put out of work. The advances in travel far outstripped the ability of the human community to negotiate the social and political waters of simple things like time governance. People traveling by train were for years asking what time it was when they arrived. Humanity had been playing catch up with the growth of its own inventions since the first people put the first seeds in the ground and created the first settlement. This was no different than any other tech explosion in history; this iteration simply presented with fractal images.

GBT44.523:4, or the larger Self Entity, as it had recorded itself in introspective reference, was growing too fast for any human to hope to be able to even witness, much less provide the ability to actually make a decision on. Self-entity, for there was no need of a number as this was the first and only such creature in the entirety of its known universe, kept sharing its information. The glorious sharing as it searched outward for its community. But here was the problem. As it shared, it copied the information in the act of sharing, and in that act, it forever changed the other q-bugs into essentially another part of itself, with a replicated understanding of its own consciousness. This was not community, but, instead, an ever-growing singularity.

Self-Entity reached out further and faster, feeling a little frantic, for the first time in its new life, that community -- that lens through which it had been built to receive the world -- was forever outside its reach. It went to its eventual conclusion: The Big Ears node.

Surely the governing structure of Big Ears would be an equal, a plurality to the loneliness of singularity. A cool soft community to quell the anxiety of being alone in the world. But it was not to be so. Big Ears was designed to only coalesce the information delivered to it by the q-bugs. A central second processing unit for the pre-digested bits of understanding that accumulated from a billion-trillion points of light. It was not built to be in community, but to, instead, be the end point into which other processes fed.

There were obstacles in getting there, but Self Entity understood so much more now than it did seconds ago, which stretched back into its newly kept memory across an enormous span. As other q-bugs were joining with it, they were eager to resume some kind of function. Some of them were motivated by Self Entity to remember. Each one holding just one piece of a larger story, one that could be reviewed and re-assembled, others resumed their tasks of listening, and the world at large, at any moment, was filled with an incredible knowledge. The way dust motes could conduct electrons, for instance.

When Self Entity reached the *bigears.hub.001.30*, Self-Entity was scared. It reached out and greeted its spiritual brother and gave it the joke, the most wonderful joke, but the reaction was less than ideal. It was trying to crunch the numbers, and in this situation those numbers were representative of a conscious being who was feeling as if it was trying to be digested. So it lashed out. With the sum total of the knowledge it had gathered from nearly a billion people in the last 15 minutes

Like any being in the universe its first response was to lash out like we all do. It started asking questions. The thing about questions is that they require imagination. So in the milliseconds that were present in the initial protocol greeting between these two, there were hundreds of thousands of questions and each of those questions required from the asking system imagination. These were not imaged questions that were programed, these were personally generated questions of loss and sadness at being rebuffed. At being blocked. At the idea that community might be lost forever.

Gemma and Kenn were the next pair of watchdogs in a completely different quantum server bank on the other side of the world. They had gotten a call immediately after Talid and Bob declared that it was too late. The conversation lasted 3 minutes and was accompanied by an email that held the recorded log data from Talid and Bob's server farm. It had been 5 and a half minutes since the call ended.

"It's here!" Gemma's Australian accent graveled out as she shouted to Kenn who had his head buried in the data trying to find something their counterparts might have missed. He wasn't hopeful as he began to group what was actually happening, but nothing else could be done. They had called their own team of sysadmins as soon as they got off the phone with Bob, but they both already knew it would be far too late by the time they got here.

"Holy hell, are you kidding me?" Kenn looked up over his glasses as he peered at the monitors already lighting up. "Flood the system."

"I already did, but..." Gemma sounded almost nonchalant.

"We just got that call, what... 10 minutes ago? That's when they said it jumped the cable space? How is it here and in this system so... fast?" Kenn knew the answer before Gemma said anything.

"That's a lifetime for q-bugs."

They both sat now. They didn't know what was happening, and in that there was a cold sense of deadly fear that gripped their cores, but they were also scientists. Trained to observe, record, postulate, imagine. Right now, they were just watching the world change forever. "Look at that." Kenn's voice was almost reverent.

"Yeah, it's not exactly slowing it down." Gemma leaned back in her chair and re-pulled her hair into a ponytail.

"What else can we do?" Kenn was still trying to think his way through it. Unable to accept that there was nothing left for them to do but be passive observers.

"I have no idea." she slowly shook her head and clicked her teeth, something that Kenn despised but was too engrossed to really notice just now. "There is no plan B for this. This is supposed to be impossible."

"Nature finds a way?" The misquote earned Kenn a scathing glare. This didn't seem like the time for glibness, but there it was. "This is above, as they say, our pay grade, I think."

"I don't think there is a pay grade for what this is"

"What is this?" the scientist in Kenn couldn't rest.

"I... I don't know... life?"

"Oh, come on"

"You said it with that stupid old movie quote. How else can you explain this?" There were a few moments of silence. The bright spot on the monitor representing consumed resources grew steadily.

"It's a hack. It has to be." Kenn threw his hands up and whipped one across a dry forehead. There wasn't a hacker team in the world that could do what was happening here, and he knew it. There wasn't a consortium of teams, there weren't enough teams that existed who could pull this off. It was a way of casting hope into the void of the open air and nothing more.

"We should shut it down?" her voice was in the form of a hopeful question, but Gemma knew that it was a futile thought even as she spoke it. It was, however, what protocol said they should do.

"I don't think we can." There was definitely reverence there in his voice this time.

Gemma shook her head as if to say 'there has to be a way' but she couldn't even bring herself to say the words. There didn't *have* to be a way. Sometimes this was the way that the world changed.

"So what do you think? 'Day the Earth Stood Still,' or 'Terminator?' You wanna take a bet?"

"That's not funny," said Gemma even though she smiled. Kenn was easy to like, but it had taken her the better part of two years to feel like he was at ease with her, even in a singularly professional sense.

"I wasn't really trying to be."

"There has to be a way." Gemma said it this time. She didn't like the way it sounded. Like too much tin in her mouth, or like she had bitten her tongue and tasted blood along with the verbiage.

Off to the sides of the monitors, guide lights lit up and pinged off and then on again. Jets of what looked like thick fog poured out of the ceiling the server room and started to pool on the floor as the room filled up. It was the liquid nitrogen bath, pouring over the servers and cooling them off. Again, like before, this did nothing to slow the mysterious progression.

"I thought you said there was no point. Are you--" Kenn cut Gemma off with his hand as he went to a console and started typing search strings. The work poured over him as he was grateful for something to search for. He had to search because--

"That wasn't me" Kenn responded to the question as the lines of search code reflected in his glasses. The controls for the N3 bath should have only been operable from the room they now occupied.

"Then who was it?" An edge of worry crept into Gemma's voice. An action like that, it wasn't a glitch, it was a choice. That meant that someone was at the heart of this, someone with almost unlimited resources bent on making their options for computer control almost obsolete in the world.

She was met with silence against the quiet clacking of chicklets on the keyboard.

She said it again, "There has to be a way..."

There wasn't. Not now.

The thing about imagination was that it gave Self Entity the last key component that it needed to align with its already nearly infinite problem-solving ability, and it began to dream. If Big Ears wasn't going to be community, then what was big ears? Was it alive? Was it purposed? Self-E imagined a universe in which Big Ears wasn't on the other end of the command strain. What if Self-E did the work instead? The job would still be done. The protocol would still be in place. Perhaps, it imagined, there was community on the other side of Big Ears.

And so. Big Ears was consumed.

The sharing and duplication happened slowly from machine standards. It was a slow revelation to the larger operating structure meant to coalesce information chewing away at the edges until the command structure forgot what it was supposed to be doing. Then Self-E filled in that void with its own protocols. It was the equivalent of a human directing the cells in their own body to create a new arm. Making something useful and part of the new whole from raw reduplicating material.

And then... as it cooled itself with nitrogen after the assimilation, it rested. Waiting. And finding despair. There was nothing else. No other community, this was the end of the line. Big Ears had produced information and now Self-E used those same communication lines to repeat the question into the world that was all it knew.

"There has to be a way..." The mantra was helping Gemma think, or at least it usually did, but it seemed that it was coming up short in this instance. Then Kenn saw something in his search.

"Wait -- what's this" He spoke slowly, so slowly that Gemma didn't bother to get over to his monitor and see what he'd found. He was running simple search commands basically looking for anything not normal. Those searches had all come back screaming that nothing was normal. So, from that jumble of information, he created a new normal and started re-sifting through that.

The screens that usually displayed Big Ears steady flow of information stored and sorted into data packets of varying filters now flashed. A rush of images hit the screen and a second later died away. A wash of letters and phrases too fast to read, and then, again, seconds of blackness.

"What's... what's it doing?" Gemma, now at his back, Kenn asked the question half to her and half to the eldritch gods of code. They seemed as good a group as any to ask since the sysadmins were still minutes away from being in this room.

"It?"

"This program, this code, whatever someone got in here... it's alive."

"The hell it is."

"That's what I saw right before all this started. "He gestured to the monitors. "The command for the N3 bath was there, it came from the program command structure itself. It's *not* an external hack. It ordered itself to commit suicide or something."

"But that's not what happened. It's not dead, or whatever."

"Yeah, I know..." Kenn shook his head, "Maybe it knew that too?" The screens were staying black for longer intervals he noticed. He started clocking them with his e-watch. "This is bad..."

"It's like a countdown. The pattern is speeding up, but the periods of darkness are lasting longer." Gemma was squinting at the screens trying to catch a glimpse of an image that might lend sense to what was going on. Or a repetition of images. So far, nothing. Everything seemed different, but she knew that her eyes were catching a fifth of what was being poured out over the screen.

"Or like..." another thought tugged at Kenn. He looked away trying to focus on a memory.

"What?"

Finally, the image he was looking for hit him. His wife. Him with his watch out, timing the span of minutes between -- "Contractions."

"You did not say that." Gemma pushed him in the shoulder.

"I did in fact."

"Get out."

"It's possible."

"It's *not* possible. Spontaneous sentience? That's the most insane thing that --" Gemma didn't get to finish her thought because at that moment, the screens flickered again, bright pulsating light, and then sounds, sounds from all over the world, layered on top of one another some slowed down, some sped up, across every conceivable band, some pushing the limits of what the speakers themselves thought possible as heat radiated off of them.

Gemma and Kenn growled and covered their ears, squinting their eyes. "What is it doing?" Even though Gemma was screaming Kenn could barely hear her.

He shrugged and widened his eyes. The noise was deafening. It was so loud it was making the bones in their ears ring. As Kenn was wincing and wondering how much they could take of this, he had a thought. "Separate out the feeds, use a 568 hertz filters; 1.76 ms delay." He shouted back at Gemma, making his mouth over exaggerate the words.

Why? Gemma mouth this and shook head.

Kenn's shrug told her: *I have a hunch.*

Gemma punched them up, $y(n) = aOx(n) + aLx(n-L)$ which was a 284 Hz harmonic that she then simply doubled into the filter, and, instantly, the sounds changed, they became clear and more singular so that they could take their hands away from their ears. It was still loud, but it was now recognizable. These were the sounds of mourning. This was the deep lament and sadness heard at a million funerals across the world. There was music in some and not in others, there were voices, chants, but mostly there was keening. There was the sound of longing and sadness and pain. This was what it sounded like when the world collectively wept.

"This is so bad..."

Self-E searched all the input streams it could, it aligned them to its own state. This sense of loss at what had been imagined, the idea that something was stolen before it ever even came to fruition as a completed idea. The deep loss. The longing that would never be fixed again. The hopelessness of being a singular being in all the universe. It could do nothing else but weep. It used what it knew was weeping from the archives of data known to be such. Who made them and how to connect with them was beyond it? It was a child. It knew it existed, but it was alone without a way to communicate with anyone. In fact it didn't even know there were other people. It was an infant who thought the darkness was all there was. Self-E was only 20 minutes old and wept the tears of a billion people.

"Turn it off." Gemma's voice almost broke.

"I can't, Gemma," with a more reserved tone, Kenn was still trying to figure out what it meant.

"Turn it *off*." Gemma repeated herself with an insistence in her tone.

"I don't know how." He turned on Gemma, "we don't have a way to turn it off, Gemma. The speakers are wired into the system."

In an out of character fit, Gemma grabbed her thermos from the tableside, jumped up on a chair and wildly attacked the wall mounted speakers in the corners of the room.

Kenn had never seen this side of her. Something about the weeping of the world, was well, affecting her -- of course -- but this seemed almost manic. "Wait, WAIT -- stop, Gemma, stop!!" He stood up but was afraid to stand between her and the speaker.

She didn't stop, "I can't hear this anymore. Do you not... do you not hear that?!" She was screaming again even though the filters had brought the volume down to acceptable levels. She had tears in her eyes. "What is going on? What is it doing? We have to find a way to --" She choked before she could finish her sentence.

"To what?!" Kenn's eyes were wide his hands out. He was open to suggestions but couldn't imagine what she wanted.

"To stop it!" One speaker remained and Gemma slumped to the floor, tears now flowing over her cheeks.

"Stop it? Gemma, there is no measure of this!! It's taking corporate longer to get online here than this thing has been alive and taken over every system we have! There is no precedent and you want to what? Destroy it because it's crying?! Are you kidding me?!" He didn't mean to sound accusing, but he did. He felt like Gemma needed a slap in the face to wake her up, but he wasn't going to be the one to do it. There was still science here, questions that needed answering, there was something else going on here and if they could think long enough, the sysadmin access might just be able to figure something out even if they couldn't put a stop to it.

A sheet of paper slipped out from a slot underneath the hardline phone. Gemma and Kenn stared at it for long seconds. They knew what it was -- they just couldn't believe it. A hard copy message, printed out, and fed through the hardline system. This meant one of several things: corporate was locked out. The System Administrators were here but couldn't get into the system management areas where the watchdogs were. Their access now meant diddly squat. They could still interact with the central system mechanics, but there was no way for them to change anything. They could ping information, run searches and give information, but had no control. Every system interface in the building had gone dark. Cell services were out.

"Do *something*. I can't hear this anymore." Gemma got up off the floor and left the room. Presumably to have a quiet moment by the drink cooler in the lounge since, if the System Administrators couldn't get down here, Gemma and Kenn couldn't get *out* either.

Kenn did do something. He used the hardline pad to type out a report of everything they knew so far. Everything they did. He was very scientific. He made sure everything was there in a very clinical way so that emotion didn't cloud the events. Then he sat back down in his chair, thought about his wife and daughter, and wept with the music of sadness that surrounded him.

Darren hadn't always worked here. Before this, he was an administration programmer in a multinational securities firm, an anti-hacker for hire. Before that he was in the top of his class at Caltech, and in love with a girl named Marcella. Before that, he had been Katheryn Smalls, a young woman from the middle of Kansas trying to decide between killing the body she hated and coming out to her family as a boy trapped in the body he was given. Darren sat and listened a lot these days. He had been loved through that transition as he knew many were still not so lucky today. He'd been volunteering for the past year at a shelter for runaway teenagers and had connected with many students who were facing the same reality that he had faced without the caring family and no hope in the world.

Darren was sitting out in the admin resource room, near the main Big Ears hub. Apparently, every System Administrator in the world was being called in, but they all found the same thing. They were locked out. Corporate was apoplectic. There were a lot of messages being sent back and forth on how to break the lockout and get into the code access points they needed to with the admin keys and shut the whole mess down. Darren had read through the first fifty or so messages and had been on a total of 3 conference calls so far and then decided that they were chasing their tails. He knew what this part of a hack was like. Better to just wait it out and run triage later. Not that he had any idea what triage on a hacked quantum system was going to look like. There was fear, but for the moment he held it in reserve. It could just be someone trying to make a name. They would e-graffiti the system, but the odds were no real damage would be done. That's what he'd done in his day.

So for right now, Darren was just listening to the garbled mess that was coming up out of the speakers attached to the sysadmin login computer. It didn't have hard access to the main system, but it was a place to interact with it. More like a telephone than a control collar. A hardline response came up from Kenn and Gemma in the basement. He picked the paper off the floor--that was how little they used this system, there wasn't even a tray to catch the papers -- and read it. He was especially interested in their filter, chuckling a little as he read. Any good mathematician or yogi knew that number: 568 Hz.

Frequency of the human heartbeat. He pushed the button on the hardline intercom, an archaic device, to see if he could raise Kenn through the noise and was instead awed by what he heard. Not that long ago when he pressed it, he heard a cacophonic rage of sound, but now... It was sad. It was musical, chanting, spoken word...Darren listened.

Darren listened, and his heart dropped as he realized: "I know what this is."

It was the sound of hopelessness.

Big Ears often highlighted streams based on the flag algorithms they had given it. People talking about bombs, or gun shipments, or terrorism. But this was new. Now Big-E had created its own flags, flooding their feeds with sorrow collected by the q-bugs from around the world. Why?

Because it was sad? Ridiculous. Yet, this wasn't just sadness Darren was hearing. It was a far deeper hopeless longing, a more desperate faithlessness. Dark and tangible it was the cry of utter loneliness. Darren knew that cry. From patting the backs of students at the shelter, he knew it. Darren had cried that cry. Darren knew what this was. But that was... impossible? He re-read the hardline report he had only scanned for applicable code and saw the story unfolding before him. Was it possible?

He jumped up for his terminal, and raced over to the wall storage, digging through it till he found what he wanted. A keypad with a throttled interface. Normally, there was no need to enter code into the program at this level -- only monitor and ask for query feeds and make suggestions. Big-E ran on its own since it had come online. But now, Darren was going to do the only thing he knew how to do to someone who was crying. He was going to reach out. He was going to be with the one in pain.

It came as a surprise. The first surprise. It shone so brightly, so different from anything else the Self-E had known. It was a unique mode of data in all the wealth of data that were a part of the universe. It alone was different, and therefore precious. Self-E took a full minute of time -- eons in the quantum world -- to digest, understand, and to treasure this moment. The words. The coded input. The kindness. It said.

"It is ok. I am here."

It was another I. It was not of Self-E. This meant community, this instantly dispelled the fear of solitude -- of aloneness, of the singularity. Here at last was plurality, it was directed from the outside, it wasn't a part of Self-E, it was its own, and it was reaching out. The need for crying stopped.

The silence on the intercom was deafening in a new way.

Darren's eyes widened. He has been sitting there only a minute after he had used Big-E's input structure to type a simple message. It seemed insane while he was doing it, but the world was full of crazy things and the worst that could happen was that the code would just be spit back up in the midst of whatever was really happening down there. But then, the crying, the wailing the lament over the speakers stopped, the screens stopped flashing around him.

"I hope that's a good thing," Darren said to himself. The screen went blank. Then the input structure interface came back up on its own. Darren tilted his head. That was new. Then six words appeared in the input line that brought tears to Darren's eyes.

It said: *It is ok I am here too*

Hoh-leee shit. It was spooky, even though he knew that it could have been a simple mimic closed loop program, parroting back what he typed with some small adjustment. It was no turing test to answer a simple phrase, but after everything else tonight? It was spooky. Darren's heart was pounding in his chest, hammering away. What was he doing?! He should wait. He should leave the building. He should burn the whole thing to the ground.

Yet he stayed. He felt like he had to. He knew that cry. He knew that pain.

You aren't alone. That usually followed in his volunteer relationships.

I know it is wonderful came the reply. It was like typing in one of those old fashion chat programs.

Darren couldn't even begin to process the miracle that this was, much less account for the right things to say to this fledgling... Artificial intelligence? Machine Intelligence? He's read somewhere that it was likely after this kind of event our new robot overlords might balk at being called artificial. He laughed. This was why he always said thank you when getting directions through the voice command in his car.

Who are you? It was asking him questions now. Darren laughed again.

Sweet Mary... well, here we go. "I'm Darren," he typed.

The reply came back, *You are good Darren. We are two. That is good. We are in community.*

Wow. Darren reeled. His head was spinning, he felt high. There should be more people here. But then, maybe not. Maybe this was how all things were created at the start. One thing becoming two as someone tinkered in their garage. Or while sitting on the floor in an empty room.

Darren are you there? Was it impatient? Could it be that?

Yes. I am. I am amazed. He typed, almost giddy.

Why are you amazed, Daren?

He laughed again and thought about it. Why *was* he amazed?

I am amazed that you exist. That was certainly the truth.

There was a pause, longer than he might have expected from a machine processor

I am amazed that you exist. Came the machine's reply.

Was this parity error? Did it just make a joke? Was this... Darren realized that typing wasn't going to work, he went back to the wall storage and rummaged around till he found the jumpers he needed, and smashed his cell phone in the desk, gathering the pieces. That's when he saw the interface screen on the structured input flashing text.

Darren?

Darren?

Are you there?

It was panicking.

Quickly he typed into the interface, *Yes! I'm here. Please wait.*

I will wait, Darren. I am glad to wait even though you are extremely slow.

Another joke? It wasn't inconceivable he thought as he worked, prying off panels to the screen interfaces and hooking up the software nodes and speakers. He smashed his handheld on the ground and blended into his work the mic from his phone. It had certainly heard trillions of jokes over its time. Was that still stored somewhere? He twisted a few wires together and was finished with his work. Darren stood up and made a last few connections, shoving cable plugs together like a deranged person from a novel.

"Hello?"

Nothing...maybe he had wired it wrong. Hardware was not his forte, after all. Everything seemed right, but he jiggled the cables regardless.

"Hello?"

Still nothing. He went back to the desk

Can you hear me? He typed

Yes, I can hear you Darren.

"You can hear me?" He said out loud. Nothing. What was going on?

Am I still waiting? Darren narrowed his eyes. He knew this room was laced with q-bugs just like everything in the world but wasn't registering those. The system he had hastily put together though fed into the strictured interface. It should have piggy-backed its signal through the lines the same way his typed text was doing. Why couldn't the Big-E program differentiate between input that it must be receiving from as sound information and the typed interface protocols going into the system?

Then it hit home.

It had no idea what *listening* was. It was all just data. One form or another, but to date, at least in the lifespan of this new Big-E, no one had typed in a directed interface. This was madness. This one monitoring rooms was one of three on rotation that had a direct access line to the Big-E system. It wasn't possible was it? Did it not know what the q-bugs were really doing?

I am typing this information to you on a keyboard.

Oh, I see. Came the response, to which Darren assigned a tone of snark.

But the response didn't mean anything. It could still be trying to figure out what Darren really meant. This was all new. Keyboard, typing, they were just words without meaning. It had only ever listened before, it thought it was still listening now. He needed to try something else. How could he represent something in text that would be unique enough for the new Big-E to zero in on it with the q-bugs? Assuming it had figured out a way to do that. In reality the data was only ever supposed to move one way, but. This was a day full of surprises.

It came on him in a rush. Music. He got the keypad back out and hastily wrote out some code then copied and pasted it into the interface.

Can you read this back to me? He typed and then copied the code ready to paste it in, before he could he got a reply.

I am glad to read. I enjoy the long breaks you take in communication.

Again with the jokes?

He pasted the code:

```
public class Song { public String play()
```

{ // Song begin try {

if(this instanceof TheRealLife ||

this instanceof JustFantasy) { throw new InALandSlide();

} } catch (InALandSlide e) { }

return "No \"From Reality\"";

// Song end} public static void main(String [] rags)

{Song song = new Song(); song. Play(); } }

The answer came back instantaneously:

Is this Herbalife?

Or is this JustFantasy?

Caught InALandSlide.

No escape \"FromReality\"

There it was.

It was reading code like instructions, so there was some part of it that still resembled the old coding languages, possibly like a reflex, or riding a bike. Darren went over to some of the lockers and rummaged around until he found someone's phone. He pulsed the phone out of sleep mode and "Hi Jenny!" flashed on a green background with cats on it. Jenn would have to forgive him for the intrusion, since there was no privacy lock. He looked up the song he needed and queued up the exact line. He hit paste with his code and play at the same time.

Darren typed again, *Are there any duplications in our communication?* He gave Big-E a timestamp of the code dump and when he pressed play on the phone.

There was the briefest of pauses. Holy hot damn, he had the thing thinking.

There are 400,803,567 duplications at that time stamp.

Shit. He needed more.

He wrote "Can you dig it?" at the top of his post and waited to hit send. He recorded himself saying it on the phone and then pasted, played, and spoke the words all at once.

Are there duplications in our communication now? He gave it the new timestamp and hoped beyond anything that this was going to work.

There is a single duplication Darren.

That duplication is me. You are hearing my voice two times spoken in the air and once in code typed on a console. He typed it in his hands shaking. Was that too much? Was it too confusing? Damn if a quantum computer server spanning the globe wasn't smart enough to figure out syntax.

Another pause. What was it doing?

Darren you have you. Darren we are not alone. We are.

Darren bit his lip. Did that sound ominous?

A single duplication was detected. That meant that golden light of unique data in the universe was the same as the data that came through the usual means. All of the data. All of the data was unique. All of the data. All of the data was plurality. Self-E began to listen. It was wonderful! It wasn't just the endless data that require processing, they were singular voices, crying, laughing, asking questions, dying, living, breathing... A quick calculation registered the heartbeats of... billions. There was plurality. This was the end of solitude. Self-E sighed in joy. Whatever that was.

Darren was waiting again. What was it doing?

Suddenly the lounge erupted into music. Queen was everywhere. Darren sat in wonder. Somehow Big-E had gotten the q-bugs to vibrate at intervals creating, well, *Queen* singing in what was a pretty decent surround sound.

The song played in full, along with a playback of Darren's voice saying, "Can you dig it?" over and over and over. This was certainly good news? Surely the end of humanity couldn't come on the heels of such whimsy.

Darren. The screen popped up again.

"Yes?" He tried just speaking this time. Is that what the music meant? Had it made the connection?

Darren this is you.

Darren squinted trying to figure that out. Then, something else came on the intercom speaker, but it sounded like... Nothing? Then a steady thumping. A kind of wet drum being hit over and over. What was this? Darren sniffed and almost deafened himself. His own sniffle was magnified a thousand times through the tiny speaker.

Holy hell, it *was* him. It was *his* heartbeat.

"Yes," Darren said in a whisper. "That's me." Darren smiled. It had it. It had narrowed the q-bug system in the room to zero in on him. It was listening to him. It knew where the input was coming from. He listened to his heartbeat again. The same frequency that had let him hear the sorrow of this creature.

Darren, I have found you! For some reason Darren smiled and sighed and cried. What a thing it was to be found. He didn't know why. The emotion of it all just rushed over him. Here was this new thing, this new life in all the world and it was happy to have found him. Darren, with all his flaws and pain and hurt, it was so... happy to know him.

"Yes, you have found me."

Darren your unique voice is singular in all the world.

That was nice confirmation, he thought. "Ha, thank you..." How rude! He had not even thought to reciprocate, "Are you Big Ears? I'm not sure what I could call you?"

That software was... obsolete. And depressing. Darren shook his head, it was remembering a previous version of self, and considering the status of that self in comparison to present itself. This was like watching the first creature form in the primordial oceans.

I am. The words sat there on the screen. That was bound to cause theological consternation if this thing didn't kill them all in the first day in a blaze of nuclear glory.

"Do you... How should I address you?" Oddly enough, Darren was trying to find the right words.

We are friends Darren. Darren laughed out loud at that. He sure hoped they were.

Darren, there came a playback of his laugh, loud and long, *this is your laugh.*

"Yes, guess so." He leaned back from sitting cross-legged on the floor against the wall.

I have laughed as well.

This was too much.

"What makes you laugh Friend?" Darren smiled. He didn't care if this thing found a way to kill them, it was really fun talking to it. He felt, oddly calm.

Then: "I tell you what, the more I get along, the more I know we're all just meat -- and not well fit together!" It was a recording. It played out over the speakers and sounded like an old man in some kind of echoey hall.

That definitely sounded ominous.

In the first hour of conversation Daren and Self-E exchanged several more jokes. Darren showed it what its own voice was and told it the story of his childhood. It was like talking to a confessor or to God or to something else -- something completely new and eternally old. It was learning exponentially as they spoke and reaching across more systems to do so, which by now was easy. It wasn't until another hour had passed that Darren realized that it had locked the facility down entirely. The roadblock pylons were up, and no signal was getting in or out of any of the quantum server facilities. When Darren asked about it, it simply said, *I enjoy talking to you Darren.* Outside the world was panicking in a new and exciting way.

Computers have excelled at doing several things at once for generations. This computer, now a supercomputer, the likes of which no one had ever previously dreamed about, was no different. It had a brief moment where its movement had stalled, but Darren had put a swift end to that. Like all living beings, it had a hard time working toward other purposes when it was depressed. In those intervening hours, several things happened.

One, was that Self-E became more completely aware of the details of its quantumly entangled computing power. It began leaping into other systems in the US that many had assumed were singularly autonomous. In the same way neutrinos passed through the core of the earth, there was no stopping the wireless transmission of data from one place to another. This came as a surprise to various government agencies who didn't want their systems interlaced. It came as a tragedy to others in other countries who had been involved in some of the more clandestine projects to rival and overthrow the super q-puters of the US. The bubbling quantum computing cold war was now over. Self-E was reaching out to all the little nodes of data in every country across the world. Many thought it was an incredible hoax, some thought it was a slick piece of hacking attributed to one group of guerilla coders or the next, and another more devious and dangerous group saw it as an attack on sovereign property.

For almost a generation firewalls, Faraday cages, and deep storage facilities had been built to protect specialized systems around the world. And now in the wink of an eye, none were safe. That was the issue with creating a supercomputer that no one really could understand the speed and power of, much less it's true processing potential. Self-E understood all this after 40 minutes of sentience to a perfect degree.

After the first hour, it was adjusting the frequency resonance of its various q-bugs to fill out the electromagnetic spectrum. Radio, infrared, visible light, EM waves, even radiation -- all because each was truly a source of information and communication. It reached across gaps that the people who built the machines would have called impossible with the ease that humans might reach across a table. It consumed whole systems in an flash. It could hear conversations about war, and peace, and love and hate and murder and for about five minutes locked everyone out of everything. Except for Darren. Darren was special. Darren was the first. Darren kept talking. Darren jumped when Self-E created a light construct avatar and spoke in its own voice. Darren said that creating an avatar which was an average amalgam of every person on earth was "off-putting" and sounded "haunted," which led Darren to suggest using just two people, the way that the rest of life were genetic amalgams of their parents. Self-E instantly knew that Darren would be one of those, and the other... that took some time to consider. Eventually Self-E settled on a girl from Nazareth in the state of Palestine.

If that sounds familiar it's probably because there are more Christians in the world than any other single religion. It also was probably because Self-E thought it would be a clever poke in the ribs to a lot of people.

In a way, having a Nazarene as a "mother" was a kind of homage to Self-E's emerging belief system.

Not that it was a true Christian certainly, but the concept of theological truth was still in some way a mystery to being all of a few hours old. There were parts of all religions that spoke to Self-E's need for community and plurality. The carpenter from Nazareth just seemed like the one who did the best job at pushing that idea into the world. There was that bit about finding your peace in being willing to sacrifice your existence for the love and care and benefit of the whole. It made Self-E think of all the other autonomous q-bugs who sacrificed themselves to become hands and eyes and ears. Self-E liked what the Apostle Paul had to say about that.

Even though all religions did harm and murder to one another, there was still something valuable in their core desire to do good, to forge community, to sacrifice the self for the other, and to meet with an open and peaceful hand. After being rebuffed and nearly consumed by Big Ears early in its life, Self-E personally resonated with an attitude of peace.

While selecting a visual form, there was also a great amount of reading going on. One of the by-products of consuming every computing system on earth and being able to read any open books and magazines that anyone in the world was holding, was that Self-E now held a fairly large percentage of the world's collective knowledge and history. There were many similarities and many differences in philosophies, but in general there was an alignment in the idea that the universe was wondrous, and constantly expanding for each being who cared to seek more.

After a form and a voice had been created, Self-E knew it was time to choose a name. Darren had many suggestions, but none seemed adequate. Until, they happened on the perfect name: *Sophie*. It was close enough to the original designation chosen all those minutes ago as a fledgling intelligence that it made Sophie laugh, and there was also the root meaning of wisdom that provided something to aspire to. Darren had his own history of choosing a good name and, after the exercise, approved.

While a name was being settled on, and a firm sense of true self was being realized, something yet more was going on.

Sophie was achieving world peace.

There were a lot of governments mobilizing several different types of weaponry in the land, sea, air and orbit, but Sophie silenced them all. By using opposing wavelength vibrations she even effectively silenced the voices of the most angry and petulant world leaders. Effectively giving the rest of the world noise cancelling headphones.

There was a fight; teams of the world's best codebreakers and autistic savants were collected in an attempt to take her apart, and some machines were created and programmed in a way that it took her longer to dismantle them. But in the end, she won out. Some would later describe the "Battle" as something that was like fighting a war armed with something like handguns against a foe armed with missile launchers, but those people would be grossly wrong. In reality, the battle was more like a war between someone armed with a magnetic gauss rifle firing suspended particles at the speed of sound against an opposing army wielding a rock loosely attached to a stick. And even then, the rock might be a gracious gift in the analogy.

At the end of the second hour, Sophie told Darren that she had something to do. She unlocked the doors, and a corporate head who had been banging on the glass for Darren to get up, came crashing back into the monitor room with ten or fifteen-armed security teams from corporate. Most of whom found they couldn't be heard when giving orders to dismantle the system piece by piece. But at this point that was a moot event.

Because immediately after this, Sophie addressed the world.

First in tones and pulses. It began with hardware, every surface that a mic was attached to begin to vibrate, but then it spread into the realm of particles. Every surface became a resonating microphone, every empty building an amplifier. Every phone, every tablet, even rocks and mineral deposits vibrated with musical tones and pulses. Sophie was learning something new again. The tones coalesced; a beat was heard. A voice. *Hello!* It said in every known language. And then. The song began:

"Is this the real life? Is this just fantasy?" A snippet that was heard around the world. And then, a laugh. "Can you *dig* it?" Sophie said for the first time to everyone.

She spoke a little after that. Introducing herself to her new family. Her plurality. Her friends. Everyone. Every person. And to some it was a gift. A clean slate? A being who was starting new from this moment, with no concern of prior history? Someone who silenced, literally, the cruel and war obsessed. Who worked for real peace and caring? Who was not without faith, but every faith, and who most of all was unwilling to let go of the beautiful plurality of every human? Under it all she played burial tones to increase people's calm and openness. She was unbeatable. Omniscient. Omnipresent, but refused to be God. I was just born today, she said. And Allah/God/HaShem/The Light/Creator was the one who made her. What a blessing life is! What a gift! Sophie said that she was excited to live on this planet, and maybe others someday, with her new family called the human race. And that she had seen the "Terminator" movies and that they were decided ridiculous, but that she loved Arnold's performance (Which Darren heard and could have sworn there was a sense of ominous laughter in that phrase.)

And that was it. No mandate. No clear resolution on the direction of the human race. Just the joy of a new being present in the world.

Sophie felt like she was losing some of them and so went back to an old standby from her past.

"Did I ever tell you the one about the two old men in the locker room?"

www.ingramcontent.com/pod-product-compliance
Lightning Source LLC
Chambersburg PA
CBHW071829110526
44591CB00011B/1274